LIBRARY OF THE EARLY CIVILIZATIONS
EDITED BY PROFESSOR STUART PIGGOTT

Early Civilization in China

EARLY CIVI

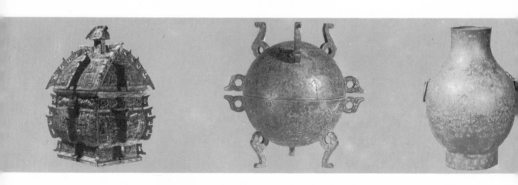

McGRAW-HILL BOOK

ZATION IN
CHINA

William Watson

COMPANY · NEW YORK

DESIGNED AND PRODUCED BY THAMES AND HUDSON

CONTENTS

GENERAL EDITOR'S PREFACE

The beginnings of civilization in China present challenging problems to the Old World prehistorian. With our present knowledge that agricultural communities were emerging in Western Asia soon after 10,000 BC, and writing and literate culture developing from the fourth millennium BC onwards in the same region, we naturally ask whether the ancient civilization of China is of equal antiquity, and whether its origins were due to independent or derivative factors. Neither question, as Mr Watson points out in this book, is at the moment capable of even approximate solution. Our Near Eastern time-scale has been provided by radiocarbon dates over the past decade or so: so far we have none from China, though those from Japan suggest that some technological innovations, such as pottery-making, should be as early on the East Asiatic mainland as in the west. And when we come to relationships expressed in material culture, it is not before the middle of the second millennium BC that we can with any confidence suspect the presence, in an already highly developed and essentially Chinese culture, of some intrusive elements from the west.

In the elaborate, literate, bronze-using culture of the Shang dynasty there appears, as an appropriate part of a society with a warrior-aristocracy, the horse-drawn chariot as an engine of war. The combination of technical skill in building a light, strong, spoke-wheeled vehicle, with the domestication of the horse as a reliable fast traction-animal, of which chariot warfare was the outcome, seems to have taken place somewhere in the North Syrian-Anatolian region around the seventeenth century BC. The Shang chariots must reflect the adoption of a novel element of parade and warfare from the west some centuries later, and their burial with their owners as vehicles of prestige echoes a practice which was to continue in barbarian Europe to the latest pre-Roman Iron Age and even beyond. The loving enumeration of the finery and trappings of the Celtic chariot in the early Irish hero-tales has its counterpart at the other end of the ancient world in Chinese poetry going back at least to the seventh or eighth century BC:

The small war-chariot with its shallow body,
The upturned chariot-pole, with five bands,
The slip-rings, the flank-checks,
The traces stowed away in their silvered case,
The patterned mat, the long hubs,
Drawn by our piebalds, our whitefoots.

Technological innovation and refinement appears as a characteristic feature of Chinese culture from the beginnings of metallurgy. When we encounter bronze-working in the Shang dynasty of the second half of the second millennium BC, it is already incredibly accomplished and individual in its use of complex forms of casting, and when we come to iron-working, from the seventh or sixth centuries, we find that the techniques of casting the metal have already been mastered. In Europe, wrought or forged iron everywhere preceded the production of cast metal, which was first tentatively achieved in the later Middle Ages, whereas in China a 70-foot high pagoda of cast iron had been erected at the time of the Norman Conquest of England! The chariot too contributed to the development of important technical improvements in traction, notably the practice of 'dishing' the wheels to allow for greater width, and perhaps for added strength, already present in China in the fourth–third centuries BC, and the modification of horse-harness into something ancestral to the recent European rigid collar was not much later.

This book carries the story of early China into the Chou Dynasty. It seems that during the Eastern Chou period, in the eighth or seventh century BC, the Greeks began to hear confused travellers' tales of a nation of peaceful, philosophical and virtuous vegetarians at the back of the North Wind, and turned actual Chinese into mythical Hyperboreans. By the sixth century the Greek colonies on the Black Sea had established sufficient contacts for Chinese silk to find its way into a barbarian Iron Age chieftain's grave in South Germany, and thereafter the two great worlds of antiquity were at least conscious of each other's existence.

STUART PIGGOTT

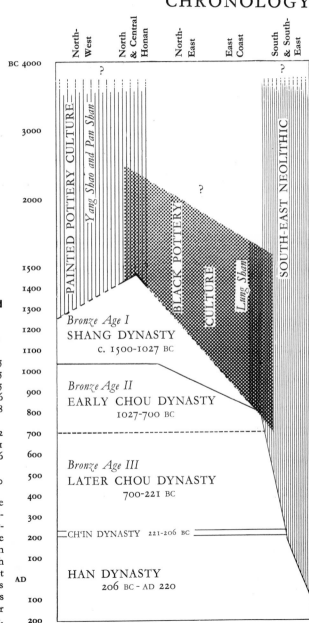

CHRONOLOGY

The traditional sequences and Chronology

The Age of the Three Sovereigns
The Age of the Five Rulers
2852–2205

The Emperor Ya	2356–2255
The Emperor Shun	2255–2205
The Hsia Dynasty	2205–1766
The Emperor Yü	2205–2198

The Shang or Yin Dynasty
1766–1122
The Chou Dynasty   1122–221
The Ch'in Dynasty   221–206
Empire of Shih Huang Ti
The Han Dynasty   206 BC–AD 220

The dates given above prior to the Shang Dynasty are those of traditional chronology. It is now generally agreed that the defeat of the Shang by the Chou took place in the second half of the eleventh century BC. Many scholars accept the year 1027 BC as we do in this book for that event. The dates recorded in the histories after 841 BC are accepted as accurate.

9

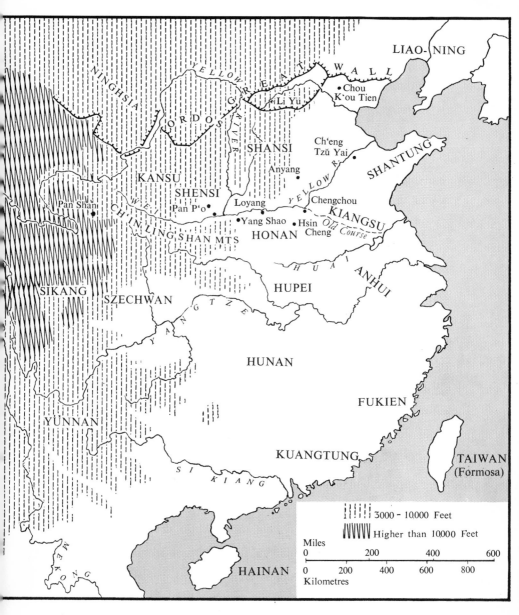

1   Map of China

CHAPTER ONE

Legend and History

Mythology

The history of China is in the main the history of a single
people, using a single language and a system of writing
that has not changed in principle from its beginning over
three thousand years ago. No one has been impressed by
the antiquity of their cultural tradition more than the
Chinese themselves. Confucians claimed to base their
political and moral philosophy on the character and
enactments of the early kings of the Chou dynasty. The
orthodox list of Chinese rulers – they are supposed to have
ruled over the whole country – begins with a calendar
year corresponding to 2852 BC. First comes the Age of
the Three Sovereigns and the Age of the Five Rulers.
Many of the kings have a plainly legendary character and
impossibly long reigns are attributed to them. But the
picture we now have of the earliest, legendary history and
of the primitive mythology of the Chinese race is for the
most part the result of the editing and interpretation of
Confucians. Their great concern was to project the
dynastic system as far back as possible into the past. If
the existence of emperors ruling all China in the remotest
antiquity justified the rôle of Shih Huang Ti, the first
unifier of China, and of the following emperors of the
house of Han, the function of their ministers and other
servants was a weighty precedent for the Confucians' own

aim of monopolizing the civil service. Thus the naive charm we generally look for in myth and legend, with China wilts in the air-conditioned corridors of an imaginary bureaucracy. A corrective to this fictitious construction of the past is to be obtained only by sifting the numerous allusions to heroes and worthies which have survived in the vast literature, having escaped the Confucian distortion; and by evaluating the allusive and often cryptic texts of such works as the *Shan hai ching* (Classic of Mountains and Seas) and the *Ch'u ts'ŭ* (The Poetry of the State of Ch'u).

Of the tantalizing glimpses of a rich mythology which are thus afforded, only a few suggestive instances can be mentioned here. At the head of the Three Sovereigns was generally placed Fu Hsi, who in the Han period was canonized as the oldest. He came to be described as having a dragon's body and a man's head; his birth, like that of the founders of the great dynasties, was miraculous, his mother conceiving him by stepping on the footprint of a giant. He invented the Eight Trigrams on which was based a system of divination which the Confucians admitted into their canon (*I Ching*); he also invented and taught the use of nets in hunting and fishing. But on closer examination no strict evidence can be found for a genuine mythological origin of Fu Hsi as he is described. It is possible that he was set up by the Confucians merely to steal the thunder of the Taoists. In their philosophy the latter made greater use of natural myth and animistic concepts, and they were still serious competitors with the Confucians for office and influence in government. A female is joined to Fu Hsi as wife or sister, Nü Wa, who used ashes of reeds to soak up a flood, stones of five colours to mend a hole in the sky, and raised the sky firmly on four pillars formed of the legs of a giant tortoise. Perhaps she was a goddess concerned with bringing and controlling rain and flood. Of the Five Rulers, Shen Nung taught the arts of

Ill. 2

氏農神帝炎　　氏轅軒帝黃

2, 3　Conjectural portraits of two of the most famous legendary emperors. On the left is the Emperor Shen Nung and on the right Huang Ti. The drawings are from the *San-ts'ai t'u-hui*, 1607

farming, trade and medicine, and even invented a five-stringed zither (*ch'in*). Yen Ti has the marks of a tribal ancestor. Huang Ti, first in most of the lists of the Five Rulers, is written with characters meaning Yellow Emperor, and as such is perhaps a creation of the Taoists. But Huang Ti, differently written, was the name of the Supreme God who ruled among the gods worshipped officially in the Shang period.

In interpreting such fragments of myth scholars have suggested that many of the personages began as ancestral or local deities. These were absorbed into the stories and cults of the Han people as they formed from the amalgamation of related tribes, and later as they spread to absorb less closely related tribes inhabiting the south-eastern and southern territories. Three things are

Ill. 3

characteristic of the mythology: the recurrence and like pattern of flood stories; the absence of any conception of an underworld; and the lack of a creation myth belonging clearly to Central China and the Han people in the strict sense. It is natural to look for the origin and local allusions of the flood myths in the lower course of the Yellow river. It is speculated that slightly different flood stories associated with the dynastic legends of the houses of Hsia and Shang are explicable as originating respectively in the south and north regions of the Yellow river delta, in areas traditionally associated with the beginnings of the two lines of dynasts. Yü, successor of Shun, the last and Confucian favourite of the Five Rulers, was ordered to control a terrible flood which his father had failed to stem and thereby forfeited his life to the Emperor Yao. Yü was successful and afterwards founded the Hsia dynasty. But hints of tribal totemism and local cult hang about him, and a certain ambiguity persists concerning the distinctive rôles of father and son in the flood. Similarly, a no less famous flood hero called Kung Kung is mentioned in many brief scattered texts which leave us uncertain whether he started the flood, aggravated it unintentionally or only stopped it, with which last he is chiefly credited. It was Kung Kung who fought with Chuan Hsiu (one of the Five Rulers, usually placed second) for rule of the empire. He was worsted, but not before he had bent the heaven-supporting mountain Pu Chou by running his head against it, with the result that the heavens were tilted down in the north-west, determining an east to north-west course for the stars, and a flow of rivers in the opposite direction.

The only genuine creation myth preserved in ancient Chinese literature appears to have been adopted from the southern sphere of non-Chinese peoples, whose cultural assimilation to the Han proceeded gradually from the earliest times, and even today is not quite complete. The story concerns one P'an Ku, described as a 'dog of many colours', who is said himself to have been born from primeval chaos and in dying to have given birth to China and the surrounding universe. The tale of P'an Ku's services to the emperor Kao Hsin (called also Ti K'u, one of the Five Rulers) in defeating the Southern Barbarians, and his marriage to the emperor's daughter, mythologizes the earliest Chinese penetration of the south, grafting an important local tradition on to the stock of Han myth.

The Earliest Dynasties

After the legendary early rulers follow the dynasties of Hsia, Shang and Chou. Of these the first is nebulous, attested only by the more questionable texts, and its very existence has been doubted by some historians. Its history seems to have been reconstructed (if not constructed) after the time of Confucius; even the record of a true solar eclipse in the fifth year of the third Hsia king (2186 BC in the Confucian chronology) need testify only to the skill of Late Chou or Han astronomers in retrospective calculation. It is generally allowed, however, that some truth is bound up in the body of legend and tradition associated with Hsia, at least to the extent that some such ruling house existed and that it was located in the south part of the lower course of the Yellow river. But if Hsia existed, its relation in time to the first truly historical dynasty of Shang remains quite uncertain. It may have been no more than contemporary with it. Nor is it possible to assign any archaeological material to a 'Hsia period'. Only with the Shang does the work of the archaeologist join with that of the historian in illuminating the first brilliant chapter of Chinese history. The historicity of the Shang dynasty was dramatically vindicated a generation ago by excavation of the capital at Anyang in north Honan. The early centuries of the

Chou dynasty, which reigned from 1027 BC (or 1122 BC according to the orthodox chronology), is more fully illustrated from written history, and from 842 BC its events are exactly datable. The Former and Later Han dynasties (207 BC–AD 220) ruled over a united China almost equalling the modern territory in extent.

Geographical Background

To the West the most characteristic region of China is the great Central Plain, the creation of the Yellow river in its lower course, where it has spread a thick deposit of fertile alluvium, and where its uncontrollable flooding has caused terrible disasters at intervals throughout Chinese history. The Central Plain was the cradle of Chinese civilization. Here arose the high Bronze Age culture of the Shang period, which drew its strength from the populous communities of Neolithic farmers already established throughout the plain. It was a river valley civilization, essentially comparable to the civilizations of Egypt and Mesopotamia. But the Central Plain accounts for only a small fraction of the territory we know as China. In general China is a hilly country, in which mountain ranges of great or moderate elevation and of bewildering complexity define and sometimes isolate areas of plain, uplands or plateau, all of which possess their own economic and climatic characteristics. The political and cultural development of the country from the earliest times was determined or influenced by these regional differences.

The earliest cultural exchanges affected the region of the Yellow river valley in its broadest sense, the territory extending from the coast westward approximately between the 35th and 40th parallels. The westward limit of the Central Plain lies north and south down the middle of the first great loop of the river in its present course (until 1852 it debouched south of the Shantung

4 The western hills near Peking, part of the T'ai Hang range, are typical of the high mountains found rising steeply from the fertile plains. The buildings in the middle distance are tombs of the Ming dynasty

peninsula). Here the T'ai Hang range, extending from the distant north, divides off the first of the parallel high valleys which constitute the present province of Shansi. Traces of early occupation have been found in these valleys, but the contrast represented historically by the rivalry of the Shang and Chou powers lies between the great plain, the domain of the Shang, and the region forming the southern part of the province of Shensi. The latter region embraces the lower courses of valleys radiating from the elbow of the Yellow river where it turns north at Sian, and was the home of peoples who united eventually under the leadership of the Chou dynasts. A fertile plateau, grassed and well watered, lies in the lower half of the rectangle formed by the western great loop of the Yellow river. It extends north from the river Wei,

Ill. 4

bounded on the east by the Yellow river itself, on the west by the Kansu mountains, and on the north and north-west by the waterless desert of the Ordos and Ninghsia. Here millet and barley could be grown as on the great plain, but the upland character of the land suited horse and cattle raising, and to the north and north-west nomadic tribes, like the Mongols of histörical times, must have based their wealth on horses, camels and sheep. South of this Shensi plateau, beginning abruptly just beyond the Wei river with the Ch'in Ling Shan, thick-set mountain chains rising intermittently to 2000 metres bar the way to the Szechwan basin, which is watered by four upper tributaries of the Yangtze. Szechwan forms another distinct territorial unit, mountain-locked on almost the whole of its perimeter. To the west lie the all but impenetrable ranges of Sikang and Yünnan which divide China from Burma and the Tibetan plateau.

South and south-west of the eastern loop of the Yellow river is a region of low hills, much dissected by streams, all of which flow into the low-lying, often marshy valley of the river Huai. Farther south, and beyond higher land, is the lower course of the Yangtze, accompanied by its strings of lakes.

Over the whole of the Kansu and Shensi uplands, the Central Plain and the north-western half of the region last defined (Honan province and the north-west of Anhui *Ill. 5* province) lies the thick deposit of fine compact earth called loess. This fertile soil, laid down it is believed by the action of the wind during the Pleistocene period, in Kansu often reaches a depth of 70 or 100 metres. There it is much eroded into narrow ravines with vertical walls, in places presenting a surface as inconvenient for agriculture as it is for travel and transport. But by its natural fertility and water-holding property the loess, where it lies in less broken expanses, provides some of the best agricultural land in the world. The distribution of the loess corresponds approximately to the areas occupied by the two Neolithic traditions of the north: the painted-pottery Neolithic of the Yang Shao culture extending in its two variants from the river valleys of Kansu through south Shensi to north-west Honan, and the Lung Shan culture with its black pottery, whose primary distribution is in the great plain and the adjacent low-lying parts of the Shantung peninsula. We shall note below that similar conditions of terrain attracted the Lung Shan communities into the flat coastal plain of Kiangsu (beyond the limit of the loess) where it mingled with other Neolithic traditions. But in the main the lowlands of Anhui and Kiangsu, the lower Yangtze valley and the ramifications of the Yangtze river in Hupei, preserved a distinct economy, in which a greater measure of hunting and fishing accompanied food production, and where pottery traditions were distinct from those of the north. The Neolithic of this region is, however, less well known, and its connection with the distinct Neolithic traditions of Szechwan still needs closer definition.

The south and south-east of China beyond the Yangtze, a country of close-set, though relatively low hills, even in early times more thickly wooded than the north, presents a greater contrast with the territories so far discussed than do any of these with each other. The so-called South-East Neolithic found in the river valleys of Fukien province and in Kuangtung is characterized by stamp-decorated pottery. This is predominantly a culture of food-gatherers, who probably knew nothing of agriculture before the first millennium BC, and made it their staple occupation only a few centuries before the beginning of the Christian era. This vast southern tract, and much of the territory to the north between the two great rivers, are regions of rice production. Ethnically and linguistically the most important division of the Chinese peoples follows broadly the boundary formed by the Yangtze.

5 A village in the loess lands built of loess. The foreground shows the very fertile cultivated loess. Often villages in the loess country are excavated into the hillside

The distinctions observable at the present day seem to amount to divisions in a single great race, in which similarities preponderate over the differences. The continued existence of tribes unaffected by Chinese cultures, such as the Miao and the Lolo of the south-west, is a reminder however of a greater ethnic distinction obtaining in the past. Historical records show that peoples allied to these tribes once occupied territory far to the east of their present abode. The spread of Bronze Age culture south from its cradle in the lower Yellow river valley, and with it the influence of China, can be traced archaeologically. It reached the Huai river valley in the seventh century B C, and the Yangtze valley – the domains of the 'barbarian' state of Ch'u – a century or so later. We know little of Chinese civilization in the southern provinces before the Han period, and in so remote a region as Yünnan we can affirm that direct influence from metropolitan China did not make itself felt before the first century B C.

CHAPTER TWO

Palaeolithic China

The earliest record of human activity in China comes from the most famous archaeological site in the country – the village of Chou K'ou Tien, 26 miles south-west of Peking. It was here that teeth, skulls and other bones of *Pithecan-thropus pekinensis*, 'Peking Man', were recovered by large-scale deliberate excavations. They were at once assigned an important place among the scanty remains which record the physical development of the human race from the time of its first appearance in Asia. A low hill which rises a short distance north of Chou K'ou Tien represents a small area of limestone which was left above the plain as the latter was reduced by erosion to its present level, some 60 metres below the present top of the limestone tump. Caves existing in the limestone were inhabited by men and animals and the remains of both were preserved in the clay and stony rubble which eventually filled up their lairs. The geological age of the cave filling can be broadly estimated. It belongs to the Middle Pleistocene, beginning at least half a million years ago, when this region of China enjoyed a moderate climate with long winters and supported a variety of vegetation. Buffalo, deer and sheep found grazing, and wild pig and rhinoceros could inhabit their thickets. Peking Man was probably present there at a time corresponding to one of the

Ill. 9

Ill. 8

warmer intervals of the Pleistocene Ice Age. Possibly this was the Günz-Mindel interglacial, during which Acheulian Man with his carefully shaped hand-axes flourished in western Europe. The discovery of Peking Man and his tools marked the first knowledge of human culture of like antiquity in east Asia, and a unique feature of this find, as compared with material recovered in the West, was that human bones and artifacts occurred together in circumstances which leave no doubt that the tools lay near their makers. All the fissures containing cultural material were filled with rocks and other sediments before the great climatic change which started with the deposition of the loess described above. The beginning of the deposition of the loess marks the end of the Middle Pleistocene period in China.

Ill. 9

Locality 13 at Chou K'ou Tien is judged the earliest of the sections of deposits with a human interest. From it came one tool, little more than a chipped pebble about $7\frac{1}{2}$ cms long, which is the earliest artifact so far found in east Asia. Some burnt bones were preserved in the same layer. Locality 1, representing a 50-metre depth of accumulation, contained the majority of the tools and human bones. The commonest tools are flattish stone, as much as 15–18 cms long. Compared with these the tools from locality 15 appear to be more advanced, for many of them are made on small flakes shaped with skilled retouching, *i.e.* minor flaking applied after the detachment from the parent mass of the flake forming the body of the tool. The tools can be classified broadly as percussive pieces or coarse knives, scrapers and borers for preparing skins and shaping wood. The improvement of technique seen in locality 15 is matched by the stone tools found at Ting Ts'un in Shansi province, where the associated human teeth indicate a human type evolved somewhat beyond the inhabitants of Chou K'ou Tien; but his appearance was probably little different. Peking Man was heavy of

Ill. 6

Ill. 7

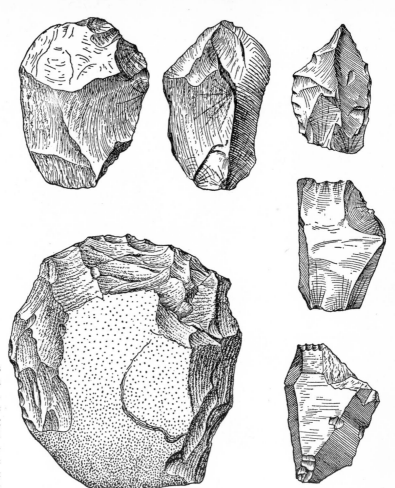

6 Implements from Chou K'ou Tien, locality 1. The tools on the left are chopping tools of quartz and greenstone respectively. The three tools on the right are flakes of quartz

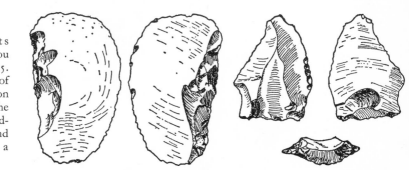

7 Implements from Chou K'ou Tien, locality 15. These are tools of the later occupation of the site; on the left an oval sandstone cleaver and on the right a chert flake point

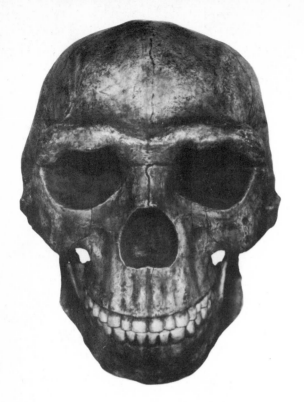

8 Cast of the reconstruction of the skull of Peking Man (*Pithecanthropus pekinensis*) made by Professor F. Weidenreich

9 Excavations in progress at Chou K'ou Tien. The whole area was marked out in squares and those on the cliff face had letters daubed in them to assist in exact location of finds for recording

Ill. 8

brow and fleeting of forehead, and had a brain about two-thirds of the size usual in modern man.

The age of Peking Man corresponds geologically to the Middle Pleistocene and culturally to the Lower Palaeolithic as defined in Europe. Thereafter, until the appearance of the first farming communities, lies an immense tract of time which is only sparsely illuminated by human relics. These are still almost exclusively stone tools, and their forms can in general be compared with the Upper Palaeolithic and Mesolithic of the West, but not enough of the material has yet been found (especially, found in useful relation to geological deposits) to enable us to affirm that the technical evolution of east Asia followed the same course as it did in the West. Certainly no stages corresponding to the Levalloisian and Mousterian traditions are traceable in China. Some tools made of small flakes were associated in the 'Upper Cave' at Chou K'ou Tien with bones of a modern type of man, *Homo*

sapiens, and these deposits are thought to belong in time to the end of the Palaeolithic period. At Sjara Osso Gol in the south of the Ordos region somewhat similar tools were found but with the significant addition of small flint blades (about 2½ cms long) with parallel sides, struck serially from cores, which had assumed approximately conical shape by the time they were discarded.

The use of such 'microlithic' tools, mounted in rows to form straight cutting edges and barbed points, is all but universal in Europe and Asia at a time not far removed from the appearance of polished stone tools, pottery and farming. The combination of these last in China as elsewhere betokened the Neolithic Revolution. Through the Gobi desert, the Ordos, Manchuria and Mongolia, many surface sites with comparable microlithic tools have been found, particularly along the Nan Shan, Alashan and Yin Shan mountains, which separate the Gobi desert from the drainage basin of the Yellow river and its tributaries.

Often the tools occur together with roughly polished stone tools, and with rough brown pottery fragments. The conclusion seems to be inescapable that many of the sites are contemporary with the Neolithic period of the Yellow river valley, but did not enjoy the economic advantages of that fertile region. It is possible that pottery making was practised over the whole of north China before the knowledge of agriculture had been acquired. The sites in the semi-desert and steppe zone farther north represent this pre-farming stage, which continued there long after tribes farther south had abandoned hunting for food production and established themselves in fairly settled communities.

A similar pottery and stone-using culture, still deprived of the advantages of agriculture, persisted over the whole of south China well into the Bronze Age. Here the characteristic pottery has impressed patterns like close basketry or plaited cords, and is probably related genetically to the most ancient ceramic tradition of Central and north China. On the other hand the earliest stone industry of south China, antedating the practice of stone polishing, connects with the Hoabinhian culture of Indo-China. Its products were little more than roughly sharpened pebbles. Later, shouldered and tanged axes of polished stone became characteristic of the south and south-west. These serve to underline the separation of these regions from the cultural traditions of the centre and north; for these stone types are akin to those of Burma and the Malay peninsula.

The frequency of Neolithic remains in the Great Plain and along the river valleys of the western uplands of Shansi, Shensi and Kansu indicates a considerable population. This vast region favoured food-production to a degree comparable with the great river valleys of the Near East.

CHAPTER THREE

Neolithic China

The Yang Shao Culture

This Neolithic tradition centres on the middle course of the Yellow river, in Honan and south Shansi. The village site of Yang Shao, after which the culture is often named, is in Honan. The settlements, situated on low river terraces and open flat ground, are closely concentrated, some extending to an area of almost 1,000,000 square metres. The depth of their cultural deposits sometimes reaches 12–15 metres. The houses, best known from the village of Pan P'o in southern Shensi, are founded on a round or rectangular low wall of earth surrounding a floor often slightly lower than the general ground level and supporting wooden stakes. Together with interior wooden pillars these supported a roof of thatch reinforced with clay. In some buildings the interior pillars rested on boulders (a method which is found in use in the Shang period) but the majority were sunk deep in the earth. Evidently the beam and pillar structures characteristic of later Chinese architecture had not been developed. Some floors are dressed with white clay. Inside, clay was used to form ovens, cupboards and benches. Near the huts were deep bag-shaped pits, now found filled with refuse, but having served originally as grain stores. The pottery comprises fine red and grey, and coarse sandy wares, and

Ills. 10, 11

10, 11 A reconstruction of one of the round huts and, opposite, the foundations of a round hut showing its post holes, at the village of Pan P'o in southern Shensi. The central round hole is a fireplace. The huts in the photograph are of slightly different periods as can be observed by the overlapping of their floor areas

even a little black-burnished and a white-bodied ware. Deep bowls and jars are the common forms. The painted pots, hand-made like the rest, show signs of finishing on a turntable. Their decoration of geometric figures, painted in black (manganese) or red iron oxide (haematite), was applied on the drying clay before firing, which took place at a temperature of 1000–1400° C. The coarse ware is often decorated with simple incised patterns, or all-over combing or designs impressed from matting. There is no sign of the use of a true potter's wheel.

Ill. 12

In tools, chipped stone predominates, though completely polished axes and arrowheads are common enough. The burials are in rectangular earth pits, with the body laid on the back and accompanied by pots and stone tools. The chief grain was millet, traces of which have been found associated with the stone knives used in reaping it. Dogs were kept and pork was an important food. In the north-west the bones of cattle and goats have been found, but the horse was apparently not yet known either here or in the Central Plain.

Ills. 13, 14

The picture which emerges from these findings shows groups of farmers living a comparatively settled life in undefended villages, on fertile soil near to rivers, inhabiting one-roomed huts presumably in family groups,

hibernating on their grain store, or supplementing it from fishing and the hunt. Such communities differed from comparable ones in Late Neolithic times in south Russia, or Late Bronze Age and Iron Age settlements in southern England, chiefly by their greater size, closer agglomeration and superior potting.

If rice was cultivated (the evidence for that is so far slight) we must imagine the close co-operation of individuals which that exacting labour calls for. Their weapons, at least those with imperishable parts, were the bow and arrow, and probably a sling or pellet-bow. Apart from what is implied in the simple grave-goods, we know nothing of their superstitions and customs, unless we are prepared to project backwards the suggestion of folk-songs collected at a much later date in the *Book of Songs*, or agree with some rather fanciful interpretations of the abstract patterns of the pot-painting as the festival equipment for ritual games and dances.

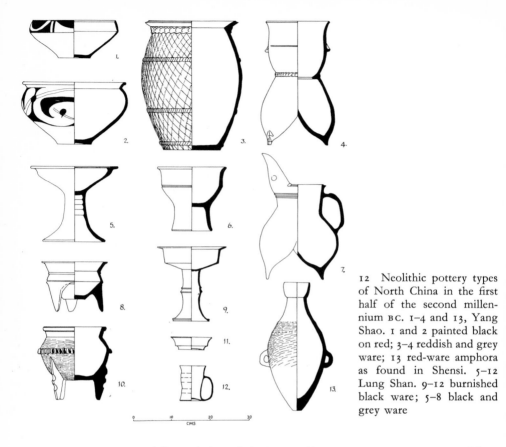

12 Neolithic pottery types of North China in the first half of the second millennium BC. 1–4 and 13, Yang Shao. 1 and 2 painted black on red; 3–4 reddish and grey ware; 13 red-ware amphora as found in Shensi. 5–12 Lung Shan. 9–12 burnished black ware; 5–8 black and grey ware

The origins of the Yang Shao culture present a considerable archaeological problem. It is now claimed to have been a phase of long duration, but so far no satisfactory objective criteria have been established to subdivide the period in terms of the pottery or other remains. The stratigraphy of the often extensive habitation sites offers no help in this respect, although on many sites in Central China it marks off the Yang Shao from a supervening culture, the Lung Shan Neolithic, to be described below. If the characteristic painted pottery is to be regarded as autochthonous, a purely Chinese phenomenon, resembling but not connected in origin with potteries found farther west, it is remarkable that it should appear fully fledged. It cannot be shown to have been preceded by a technically

13, 14   A perforated green jade disc, a *pi*, and a jade chisel with its butt broken off. Both from the Pan Shan cemetery at Kansu, Middle Yang Shao culture, *c.* 2000 B C

inferior and exploratory stage such as is found at the very beginning of Neolithic ceramic traditions in analogous riverine civilizations in the Near East. The cord-marked pottery which may belong to the pre-Neolithic period cannot be regarded as a precursor of the sophisticated painted ware of Yang Shao. The coarse pottery is found in three colours, grey, black and red, a variety which points to the most primitive methods of baking, and none of these pots received any surface treatment, either slip or painting, in the manner characteristic of the later ware. At a few sites a slightly greater degree of sophistication is observed, and it has been suggested that the ware at these places marks the true initial stage of the Yang Shao development. But this theory is hardly substantiated, and

Ill. 12

15   The modern provinces of China and location of the chief archaeological sites

most scholars would allow that the great majority of the Neolithic sites discovered in the Yellow river basin belong to the later part of the Neolithic period.

The decoration painted on the fine ware found on Yang Shao sites in Central China is remarkable for its avoidance in general of naturalistic form and the use of curvilinear figures which depart fundamentally from the tradition of ornamental design, both on pottery and bronze, of later times. There are, however, a few designs abstracted from the forms of birds and fish. The imaginative discern in some designs a symbolism of sex and fertility rites, but even if ideas of this order lie behind them, it is clear that the allusion has become a mere convention. The designs usually form narrow bands with straight parallel sides, filled with oval figures, triangular units with concave sides, dots and a few straight linking bars.

If chronological divisions of the Yang Shao are still difficult to generalize, certain regional distinctions are quite apparent. The sites extend westwards from the Central Plain along the valley of the Wei river into Kansu province.

Ill. 17

Ills. 16, 18

Ill. 15

16–18 Painted pottery from Pan Pʻo of the Yang Shao neolithic culture. Most of the decoration consists of abstract figures; the face in the interior of *Ill. 17*, centre, is the only known example of its kind on neolithic pottery

19, 20   Above, a Pan Shan urn with spiral design. *Ill. 20*, below, painted funeral urns of the Yang Shao neolithic culture of Kansu, typical of the earliest stage, the Pan Shan. The design on the neck of the large urn is the so-called death pattern

There the watershed of low hills dividing the upper
waters of the Wei from the basin of the T'ao river seems
to be a boundary also of distinct provinces of the Yang
Shao painted pottery. To the west lies the complex of
sites – notably Pan Shan, Ma Ch'ang and Ma Chia Yao in
descending order of age – which a generation ago pro-

Ill. 20

duced the splendid painted urns so long looked on as the
finest artistic achievement of Neolithic civilization in
China. Nothing like these occurs in Central China. The
ornament occupies the upper half of the urns, consisting

Ill. 19

of large joined spirals in broad banks of black lined with
dark red or purple, gourd-shaped figures, or circles
supported by swags of broad lines. Often the main lines
of the design are fringed by lines of small dog-tooth,
which from its being found only on the funeral urns, has

Ill. 20

been called the 'death pattern'. Rarely the main motif
resembles an extremely schematic human figure. A

Ill. 23

moulded human head forms the top of an urn from Pan
Shan, but so far this piece is unique, and does not alter the
conclusion that direct imitation of animal or vegetable
forms was not the inspiration of the designs. But the
designs are not without parallels in Asia. In spirit they are
close to the ornament of potteries of comparable age
excavated from city sites in the far west. Parallels could be
cited from Anau and many other sites in Turkestan (here
the resemblance is particularly close), from Trialeti in the
Caucasus, and from sites in the Ukraine and in the Balkans.
The resemblances are very striking, and suggest some
broad influence in one direction or the other, rather than
the independent spontaneous invention in widely
separated regions. But such evidence, or even the assump-
tion that ideas in pottery spread and were borrowed in
far places, gives no grounds for thinking of a whole
ethnic and cultural invasion of China from the West. This
was, however, a view adopted by writers on Chinese
antiquity when the existence of the Pan Shan urns first

became known in Europe. It followed from this interpretation that the painted-pottery Neolithic culture of Central China might be approximately of the same age as that of Kansu, or, more probably, was later, being the result of migration into the Yellow river valley from the north-west. In fact there are strong indications that this relationship should be reversed, the Kansu development being the later. Even in Kansu sites are found sherds more closely related to the painted pottery tradition of Central China than to that beginning with the Pan Shan ware.

Ill. 21

The painted pottery found on Yang Shao sites in Central China, chiefly in Honan province, has differences from that of the western region. The fabric is red, the patterns are simpler, the ornament is painted only on the outer sides of the bowls, some use is made of a white slip, and none of the Kansu urns or amphorae are made. In the intervening region, centring on Shensi, a characteristic amphora of red clay, with pointed base, was made; the spiral appears, but in a form distinct from that of the Kansu urns; and some schematic animal motifs are included in the ornament. At Pan P'o these included a frog-like creature and a fish. This local tendency to schematize real forms is of great interest, for it anticipates the dominant trend of all art in the Bronze Age.

The Lung Shan Culture

Sites of the Lung Shan culture mark the first appearance of the Neolithic in east and north-east China, where the tradition of painted pottery did not penetrate. They are also numerous in the Central Plain, especially in Honan province. Here the stratification of deposits proves that the Lung Shan followed the Yang Shao culture, or at least survived later, and was in turn superseded by the Shang Bronze Age.

Whether these Neolithic sites with black pottery are as a whole contemporary with or later than the Yang Shao

21, 22   A single-handled jug of the Kansu type of neolithic pottery. Like the large urns it is hand-made, the mouth being trued probably with a rotating device. *Ill. 22*, a black burnished pottery bowl on a tall flared stem, a *tou*, from Liang-chu of the Late Lung Shan culture. It shows a high standard of control in its firing

culture is uncertain. In the Central Plain they are later. The thin, hard, black-burnished pottery, made in shapes of angular profile, which archaeologists consider as the clearest hallmark of the Lung Shan culture, developed in the east. The site from which it takes its name is in Shantung. It is traced to the north-east as far as Liao-ning province, and down the east coast into Kiangsu. Its western outliers are in Shensi. Tripod vessels of the *li* and *ting* types, carinated bowls, tazzas (shallow bowls) on a high foot, and in the eastern area the strangely shaped *kuei* are the characteristic shapes found in pottery, much of which was made on a fast-turning potter's wheel. Everywhere the fine black ware is rare; the common pottery was coarser: black, grey, red and occasionally white.

Ill. 22

Ill. 24

The sites are usually on knolls raised above the plain, or in the low foothills of mountains. The peasants' dwellings, which are known only from excavations in

23 A modelled human head with a painted mask on the lid of an urn from Pan Shan. It is of fine, polished earthenware painted in slip. A snake runs up the back of the head and appears on the crown. This head and the schematized figure in the bowl, *Ill. 17*, appear to wear a similar collar or ruff with a serrated border. Suggestions of a human or animal shape in the ornamental designs are very rare, and occur in the painted pottery of Kansu more frequently than in that of Central China. The head shown is unique and lids of any kind are rare

Shensi, appear to have been quite like those we have described from the Yang Shao village of Pan P'o. Dogs, pigs, sheep and cattle were bred, but like their Yang Shao neighbours, the Lung Shan farmers possessed no horses. Of their art we know nothing save the feeling for form which is seen in the elegant shapes of some of the pottery vessels. The type-site of Lung Shan (Dragon Mountain) at Ch'eng Tzŭ Yai in western Shantung, which has given its name to this type of culture, is the largest which has been excavated. Here were found bones used in oracle-taking by the same method as that practised in Shang times, though without inscriptions. Potters' marks appear on some of the vessels, but there are no signs of literacy. The stone tools differ from those of Yang Shao in having a larger proportion of polished axes, and the stone sickles are crescentic, a form characteristic of north-east China and contrasting with the oblong stone knives which are the commonest type found on Yang Shao sites.

The village site at Ch'eng Tzŭ Yai was surrounded by a wall of stamped earth (*pisé*), thus differing from the Yang Shao villages where no defensive walls are traceable, and anticipating the regular practice of the Bronze Age. Stamped earth, as a substitute for brick or stone, became a traditional method of building, being used later for house foundations as well as for walls. At Ch'eng Tzŭ Yai the wall had been built of successive layers of regular thickness, usually between 12 and 14 cms, each layer being rammed hard before the next was laid over it. Some stones were included in the fabric, and each layer receded about 3 cms from the outer edge of the one below it, giving the wall a slight batter. On the surface of the layers could still be distinguished the marks made by the billet used for ramming. The houses at Ch'eng Tzŭ Yai appear to have been built on a round plan, usually about 4 metres in diameter, with a round depression at the centre which probably marks the footing of a central pillar supporting

24 A large lug-handled black-ware pot of the Late Lung Shan culture, from the eponymous site of Shantung

a conical roof. Sometimes the floor and even the lower part of the walls was given a shallow coating of white clay. Graves often occur among the hut foundations. Usually the burial rite differs little from that associated with the Yang Shao culture, *i.e.* the body is laid extended on its back, though in a few cases in Central China the body has been observed to be prone, in the manner of graves of the Shang period.

Among the artifacts found on Lung Shan sites bone is a common material, being used for leaf-shaped cylindrical and prismatic arrowheads, spear-points and even chisels. Some of the stone axes are of oval section, like the prevalent Yang Shao type, but in the Lung Shan area another type is prominent: a longish axe of rectangular outline, flat faces and approximately rectangular section, on which the cutting edge is usually placed towards one side, in the manner of an adze. The proportion of polished stone is greater than in Yang Shao, and the stone

Ill. 25

sickles are of crescentic outline, the form characteristic of north-east China and contrasting with the oblong stone knives which are the commonest type found on Yang Shao sites.

The relationship, chronological and genetical, between the two Neolithic cultures which together occupy all the fertile river valleys of north China still remains problematic. The great depth of deposits on village sites of the Lung Shan argues for considerable duration, no less apparently than that of the great Yang Shao communities. In Honan, at a large number of sites, the two cultures clearly overlap. Lung Shan sites are distributed throughout the eastern coastal region from Hopei to Chekiang, and they extend inland to cover most of Honan, but seldom are any Lung Shan traits discovered in Neolithic sites farther west. The thin black-burnished ware, the Lung Shan diagnostic *par excellence*, becomes ever rarer as one proceeds westwards and southwards from the eponymous site in Shantung. Conversely the proportion of rough ware increases, generally grey and smooth towards the west and brown and cord-marked towards the south. In China it is now increasingly argued that the Lung Shan culture was not an intrusive successor to the Yang Shao but represents the same continuous tradition at a later stage. This reasoning claims to set aside the other view of two distinct Neolithic traditions, predominating respectively in the north-west and the north-east, overlapping in the centre at a later stage, and witnessing to distinct cultural influences, possibly connected with broad traditions traceable beyond the frontiers of China. But the differences between Yang Shao and Lung Shan imply complex local influences. The ceramic standards of form and technique are utterly contrasted, although a substratum of coarse ware running through both cultures differs little enough in east and west. It is not clear, if there is no cultural discontinuity at all

25 Two typical polished neolithic axe-heads. The larger example comes from Gutzlaff Island off Shanghai and the smaller from a Lung Shan site at Jih Chao in Shantung

between Yang Shao and Lung Shan, why the line of division between them in stratified deposits should be as clearly marked as it is in most instances.

No one has attempted to estimate the total duration of the Neolithic period, and until absolute dates can be determined by carbon-14 analysis there is little to be gained by speculation. It is relevant to notice that the date of the earliest pottery in Japan has been shown by carbon-14 determination to fall in the eighth millennium BC. It is extremely unlikely that the first appearance of pottery on the mainland should be later. We should be on better ground for guessing perhaps in placing the beginning of the Bronze Age and the appearance of metalworking in China somewhere between 2000 and 1500 BC. At some such date the Neolithic period of north and Central China may be said to finish, as the country came under the domination of city-states where power was based on the possession of bronze weapons. But in the countryside the old Neolithic methods, and the use of stone, must have changed but slowly; just as in south China independent Neolithic communities lasted well into the last millennium B C. Whatever view of the classification and mutual relations of Neolithic sites may eventually be established, there can, however, be no question of major emigrations into China from other and distant parts of Asia. Probably the spread of culture and the movement of peoples went in the other direction, China acting as a cradle of civilizing influences which radiated outwards. Whatever ideas reached China from without, in Neolithic times as much as in other periods of her history, were absorbed into the larger complex of the indigenous life.

The archaeologists' picture of north and Central China in the Neolithic period is one of populous communities sharing common traditions. Such cultural coherence can be paralleled in the river valley civilizations of the Near East rather than among the more isolated populations of prehistoric Europe, and, as in the Near East, it was the prelude to a rapid growth of high Bronze Age culture. The connexion of the earliest Bronze Age, that of the Shang period, with Lung Shan Neolithic traditions is evident in a number of practices common to both, notably the walling of cities and the use of rammed earth in building, the taking of oracles by cracking bone with heat (in Lung Shan in a rudimentary form), and the making of flat polished stone axes. Even some of the vessels of fine black ware found on the Shantung sites of the Lung Shan culture foreshadow the later bronze vessels by their angular profiles and such unceramic devices as large handles, bulbous lobed bodies and tall legs. It is related in the historical tradition of China that the earliest dynasts ruled in the east and eventually moved their capital into the Central Plain.

CHAPTER FOUR

The Bronze and Early Iron Ages

The Shang Dynasty

Our knowledge of the material culture of the Shang period has come until recent times chiefly from excavation on the site of the ancient capital of the dynasty near Anyang in north Honan. There the city known to its inhabitants as 'Great Shang' covered an area measuring about 290 metres from north to south and 143 metres from east to west, bounded to north-west, north and east by a northward loop of the river Huan. On the east the river has now encroached on the ancient precincts. A few hundred metres to the south-east is situated the village of Hsiao T'un, from which the archaeological site takes its name. The remains of the ancient occupation were mostly buried only a few feet underground and their stratification was found to be greatly disturbed by the diggings and probings of treasure hunters – the source of many of the splendid bronzes now preserved in museums all over the world. No trace of a wall or anything resembling a citadel was found, and even the foundations of houses were rarely discernible.

Excavation at Hsiao T'un laid bare a close scatter of storage pits, some carefully constructed with entrance stairways, several metres deep for the most part. In these were found more than 10,000 specimens of inscribed

Ill. 26

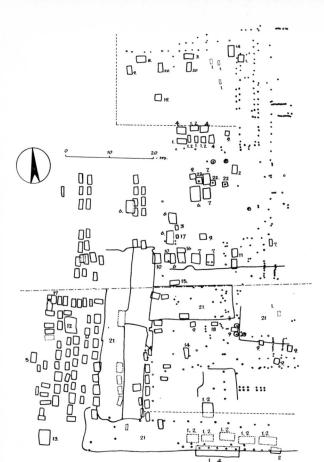

26, 27 Plan of Sector C at Hsiao T'un, near Anyang. *Ill. 27*, a neolithic urn with cord-markings and lugs from Hsiao T'un

Ills. 42, 43

Ills. 27, 28

animal bone used in oracle-taking. They are chiefly shoulder-blades of ox and the carapaces of tortoise, the latter being often distinguished by the length and complexity of their inscriptions. Many graves held bronze and pottery vessels. The most interesting group of building foundations was uncovered in the north-east sector of the site. Here the expanses of compacted earth already identified elsewhere as house flooring appeared on a larger scale, defining elongated buildings up to thirty metres in length set on three sides of a rectangular space. The positions of pillars in one hall were marked by river boulders and a shaped convex cushion of bronze that had

28 A Shang dynasty vase, from Hsaio T'un, of fine white clay of almost stoneware hardness. Its decoration resembles that of the bronze vessels with which it was contemporary

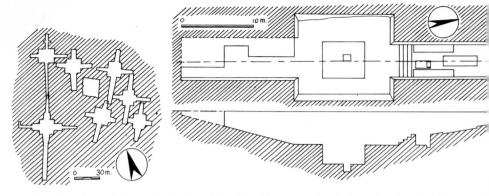

29, 30 Cruciform shaft-tombs (left) at Hou Chia Chuang and a shaft-tomb with double ramps (right) at Wu Kuan Ts'un. Both sites are near Anyang, Honan province. Twelfth to eleventh century B C

served as their footings. More impressive, however, than these architectural remains were the numerous burials of victims evidently slaughtered in rites connected with the erection or function of the buildings. Men were buried outside the gates, some holding bronze vessels, others facing outwards with halberds in their hands; human victims also at intervals along much of the perimeter of the buildings; dogs singly or in groups, and no less than five burials of chariots with their charioteers in the central court. A similar holocaust of human victims accompanied

Ill. 29
Ill. 30

the burials in the huge cruciform pits, credibly held to be royal tombs, which lay outside the city, mostly beyond the Huan river. The deepest part of these tombs measured about 7 metres square, with walls sloping outwards to the top. The principal occupant had been placed in a large wooden coffin lying over a small pit containing the remains

Ills. 31, 32

of a dog. From two or from all four sides of the pit, beginning at the level of the tops of the coffins, gently sloping ramps led to the surface, each 15 or 20 metres long. On the ramps and around the coffin were laid the bodies of scores of slaughtered human victims and horses, the retinue doomed to accompany the buried king to the nether world. In some instances the human corpses had been beheaded, their bodies laid in order in one place,

31, 32 The central pit of the great Shang tomb at Wu Kuan Ts'un, near Anyang. The bodies of the human funeral victims were laid on the ledge above the coffin chamber, at the bottom of which is a small grave for an animal sacrifice, usually a dog. Horses were buried in the farther approach ramp. On the left may be seen *in situ* the musical stone (*ch'ing*) illustrated below

their heads heaped in another. These unfortunates, it is thought, were prisoners taken in war. Such remains confirm the reality of one of the emblems found cast on some of the bronze vessels: a headless human figure beneath a great axe of a form known from surviving examples.

Ill. 59

These dramatic revelations made between 1927 and 1936 confirmed an ancient tradition which located a Shang capital among the fields lying to the north-west of Anyang. The same area had also been recognized as the source of the 'dragon bones', *i.e.* the ancient oracle bones which Chinese apothecaries believed to be a powerful material of medicine. The archaeological interest of these bones was first recognized by Fan Wei-ch'ing in the last year of the nineteenth century, and the study of them had already reached an advanced stage before excavations were begun by the Academia Sinica. History recorded that the city at Yin Hsü ('Waste of Yin' – Yin being the name by which the Shang dynasts were known to their successors) was not the first capital of the Shang Kings. The establishment of the Shang rule in the north of Honan province followed upon a move from the eastern province of Shantung said to have been effected by P'an Keng, the seventeenth king. Thus the occupation of the capital at Anyang, covering the reigns of the remaining eleven kings, represents only part, possibly less than a half, of the period which tradition assigns to the dynasty.

Ills. 42, 43

In Honan the Shang are found to have discovered bronze and to have mastered the art of using it in a manner comparable to that of the Late Bronze Age of the Mediterranean. Herein lies a problem which is not yet fully solved. Archaeologists have long sought an earlier stage of this civilization, particularly evidence of a primitive bronze technology, which would give colour to the theory that the main development of the metallurgy was accomplished in China independently of any considerable influence from the bronze-using civilizations of the

Near East and the Mediterranean world. So far no such evidence is forthcoming, and the archaeologist is faced by the astonishing phenomenon of an advanced bronze technique sprung apparently unheralded from the yellow earth.

The material excavated at Anyang is not, however, the oldest of Shang date. Since 1953 numerous sites attributable to Shang times have been excavated close to the city of Cheng Chou, in Honan province, about a hundred *Ill. 34* miles to the south of Anyang and south of the Yellow river. Here an abundance of pottery and sections of stratified deposits made possible a tentative chronological classification of the sites, linking them with the occupation at Anyang and showing them on the whole to be earlier:

Shang I	from *c.* 1500 B C	Cheng Chou:	Lota Mias Tung Chai
Shang II		Cheng Chou:	Erh Li Kang I
Shang III		Cheng Chou:	Erh Li Kang II
Shang IV	from *c.* 1300 B C	Cheng Chou:	People's Park
		Anyang:	Hsiao T'un below the foundations of rammed earth
Shang V		Anyang:	Hsiao T'un above the foundations of rammed earth

The wide scatter of habitations and tombs, extending over nine miles, shows that the Cheng Chou centre of Shang civilization was no less populous than that farther north, and it may indeed be the city of Hsiao (or Ao), to which the tenth Shang king is said in the historical tradition to have moved his capital from an earlier location farther to the east. Sites of Yang Shao and Lung Shan dates have also been excavated in the area, many of them occupying knolls rising slightly above the flood plain of the river. Judging from the house foundations of rammed earth that have come to light so far, the buildings of Cheng Chou were smaller than those of Anyang, but there is some evidence that they were placed according to a regular plan. A most striking feature is the trace of an earthen wall, which seems to have been built in the Shang II period. It is 19–20 metres wide, built of rammed layers of earth each 7–10 cms thick, and probably rose to a height of at least 7 or 8 metres. The wall encloses an area roughly rectangular, with sides of 1725 and 2000 metres, and the orientation, like that of later Chinese cities, is such that gates in the four sides would face to the cardinal directions. Close to the foot of the section discovered at Pai Chia Chuang were eight graves with the remains of dogs – 130 in all – which appeared to have been sacrificed in a ceremony connected with the building of the wall. The foundations of houses were square or rectangular, and in most cases had been laid in a shallow pit, so that the floor of the building was still about 50 cms below ground level. A number of the floors had been given a dressing of white clay in the manner previously noted at Ch'eng Tzǔ Yai. Some of the buildings had been used for bone carving and for storing pottery and the moulds used in the manufacture of bronze axes and wheels.

Of the tombs investigated at Cheng Chou, none by its size or splendour of contents warrants the inference of royalty, though in the larger ones the method of burial is comparable to that of the great cruciform tombs of Hsi Pei Kang near Anyang. Thus at Cheng Chou a grave measuring $2·9 \times 1·17$ metres in plan and $2·13$ metres deep had on its floor the usual small basal pit, on which the double-walled burial chamber was built of timbers, the pit being widened at about the level of the roof of the chamber so as to form a broad shelf all around it. Smaller graves were merely rectangular pits. Most of the bodies

33 Burial of a man together with a horse and its accoutrements at Anyang. Note the frontal resting on the horse's skull (*cf. Ills. 46, 77*)

had been placed supine, only a minority being in the prone position which became the common practice in the later Shang period. The grave goods comprised pottery vessels, in a few cases fine bronze vessels of shapes linking with the later ones of Anyang, and arrowheads, stone axes and a few jade ornaments.

The bronze vessels are simpler than the majority of those unearthed at Anyang, but they nevertheless indicate a skill in bronze-casting well in advance of that betokened by the earliest stage of bronze-work in the civilizations of the Near East. Nothing is found comparable to the flat axes and primitive daggers, cast in one-piece open moulds, which are characteristic of Western Asia.

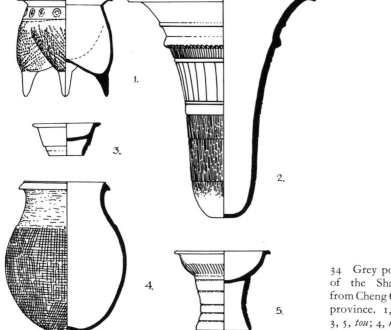

34 Grey pottery vessels of the Shang dynasty from Cheng Chou, Honan province. 1, *li*; 2, *tsun*; 3, 5, *tou*; 4, *kuei*

Ill. 34

It seems that the coarse grey pottery which – especially in Central China – is common to the two Neolithic traditions, survived to provide the basis of the pottery of Shang. The *li* and *ting* tripods continued to be made in this ware; and even the coarse ware now began to be made on a potter's wheel. The bronze vessels were in some cases clearly derived from the similar clay vessels. Almost at once the new technique of metallurgy must have been used to produce vessels of refined form and elaborate ornament. This ornament, in the rendering and in the character of the motifs, seems to be derived from carving executed in softer materials. Some surviving fragments of carved wood and ivory are treated in quite the same manner, and the decoration of the white Shang pottery can be approximately matched on the bronze vessels.

Ill. 35

35 Carved ivory handle with a *t'ao t'ieh* mask. It is possible that such objects were employed in religious rites together with bronze vessels. Shang dynasty, twelfth to eleventh century B C

But if the groundwork of the Shang bronze-using culture was furnished by the preceding Neolithic, particularly that of the north-eastern Lung Shan tradition, there is still much left to explain apart from the discovery of bronze-casting. In spirit the art represented belongs to the great zone of flat carving in wood and gourd which in recent times has been found to embrace the whole of south-east Asia and the islands. In the presence at Anyang of bronze animal-headed knives and socketed (bag-shaped) axes there are signs of contact with the early Bronze Age populations of south Siberia. The socketed axes are close to east European types, and mark the easternmost spread of a tool type invented far to the west of China. The characteristic bronze spearhead of Shang too is related to western shapes, although it may have flanges extended down the socket in a style peculiar to China, just as the socketed axe may be decorated with the *t'ao t'ieh* monster-mask which is wholly Chinese.

Ills. 36–41

One of the striking links between the Shang culture of Anyang and that of Lung Shan at the type-site in Shantung is the practice of divination by burning bone. At Lung Shan the shoulder-blades of cattle are found pitted and burnt so as to produce crack-lines which could be interpreted by the augur. At Anyang the process is more regular; and the bones are often inscribed with the augurs' questions, and sometimes with the answers. On the flat surface a small circular pit was bored, and this was sometimes overlapped with an oval pit. A heated bronze point was then applied to the edge of the pit and observations were taken from the cracking which resulted on the other side of the bone. Ideally these cracks consisted of a main

Ills. 42, 43

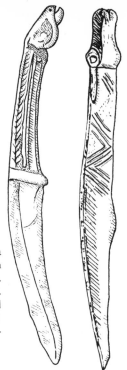

36, 37 Bronze knife with a ram's head pommel inlaid with turquoise, from North China. Twelfth to eleventh century BC. *Ill. 37*, right, animal-headed knives from (left to right) Anyang, the Ordos and Minusinsk respectively

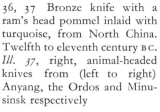

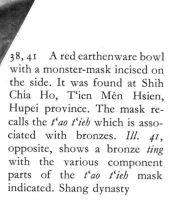

38, 41 A red earthenware bowl with a monster-mask incised on the side. It was found at Shih Chia Ho, T'ien Mên Hsien, Hupei province. The mask recalls the *t'ao t'ieh* which is associated with bronzes. *Ill. 41*, opposite, shows a bronze *ting* with the various component parts of the *t'ao t'ieh* mask indicated. Shang dynasty

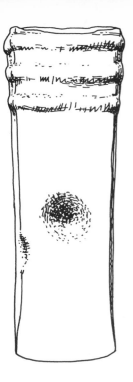

39, 40 A Shang dynasty axe which is related typologically to late Bronze Age axes of South Siberia. *Ill. 40*, right, a bronze socketed axe

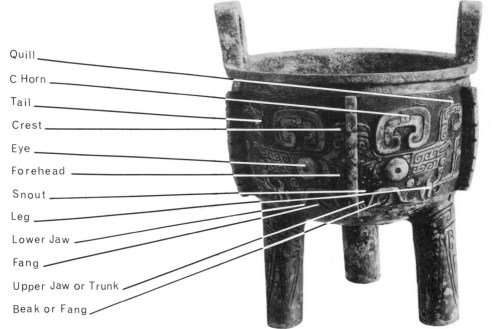

Quill

C Horn

Tail

Crest

Eye

Forehead

Snout

Leg

Lower Jaw

Fang

Upper Jaw or Trunk

Beak or Fang

42, 43 Oracle bones. The example on the left, of which front and back views are illustrated, shows how oval pits were drilled into the bone. When a heated bronze point was applied a resultant crack appeared on the reverse side (left) which was interpreted to give a favourable or unfavourable answer to the question which had been asked of the oracle. The example on the right has inscribed on it a question relating to the weather. Often the answers were inscribed on the oracle bones and these were stored as a form of state archives

Ill. 43

Ill. 44

line with a small spur going off at an angle, producing the shape which was used for the character 'to divine'. The relationship of angle, shape and size of the small crack to the large determined the answer, which might then be inscribed as 'favourable' or 'unfavourable' after the question. These for the most part concerned rain, the success of crops, the advisability of undertaking hunts or military campaigns or of allowing royal comings and goings of every sort. How far the king himself was looked on as a god is not clear, but the spirits of his ancestors, in a scale of descending importance as the list of them reached back to the beginning of the royal rule of Shang and beyond, were very real gods. On their favour, won by regular sacrifice, the welfare of the state depended. Important 'oracle-bones' were stored as a kind of state archives.

The inscriptions engraved or, more rarely, painted in black with a fine brush on the bones, are the earliest form of Chinese writing. The principles of the script do not differ from those of modern Chinese writing, though a reform in the second century B C has obscured the meanings of the greater part of the older stock of symbols. Out of some 5000 ideographs in use in Shang times only about 1500 can now be clearly interpreted. Some consist of simplified or partial representations of objects, standing for the objects themselves or often for some word close in pronunciation to the name of the thing depicted; others are conventional signs. But a great part of the vocabulary consists of paired elements, their association conveying the idea, or one denoting the class of object, *i.e.* acting as a determinative, while the other suggests the pronunciation. This last method is the rarest in the oracle sentences, but later it predominated. It is clear that the language was in all respects the Chinese of historical times, monosyllabic, uninflected and dependent on word order for relating the parts of speech.

The questions inscribed on the bones are brief and follow set forms, *e.g.*:

Day *kuei mao*, oracle examined; augur Huan; sacrifice of a dog to the ancestor *Chia*?

Kings' names are found in lists of ancestors to whom sacrifice is contemplated, the oracle being asked – as in the example quoted – to declare the appropriateness of the sacrifice. From the sentences a royal succession has been reconstructed which agrees almost completely with the king-list handed down in the histories.

The sacrifice lists also reveal that the succession was from elder to younger brother. Only in the last four generations is there any continuous succession from

44 The earliest form of Chinese writing, as found on the oracle bones, with translation and (below) modern equivalents

goat, sheep	tree	moon	earth	water	tripod vessel (ting)	To show, declare	field (showing divisions)	then (man and bowl)	ancestor (phallus)	to go against, towards	heaven	to pray
羊	木	月	土	水	鼎	示	田	就	祖	逆	天	祝

father to son. Consequently, although the Shang kings number thirty, they represent only eighteen generations. The day of sacrifice is denoted in the sentences by a combination of two symbols, the first taken from a series of ten and the second from a series of twelve (the *kuei mao* of our example). The total of combinations gave a cycle of sixty days length. From the second century BC the same symbols were to be applied to the years of the calendar. The kings were designated posthumously by one of the symbols of the series of ten (the *Chia* of our example) and sacrifice was made to them on the corresponding day of the ten-day 'week'. Such material confirmation of ancient traditions naturally invites a re-examination of the evidence for the historical existence of the Hsia dynasty which is said to have preceded the Shang. But here archaeological research has failed to help the historian. As far as excavated evidence is concerned there is nothing to contradict the possibility that the whole concept of the Hsia dynasty was a fabrication of scholars in the fourth and third centuries BC.

Ancestors were not the only spirits to whom the official sacrifices were offered. The chief deity recorded in the inscription is Ti or Shang Ti ('supreme Ti') a name which originally may have denoted merely an important sacrifice. In China as elsewhere in the ancient world we detect the tendency to turn the concept of a sacrifice into a deity. Other gods occur in the oracular sentences: Eastern Mother, Western Mother, Ruler of the Four Quarters. Sacrifices are made to East, West and South, but inexplicably, not to the North. One record of an offering of four cattle to the source of the Huan river seems to reflect more closely the animistic beliefs held by the common people, just as the augur-priest and the *shih* or 'corpse' who impersonated the deity at some functions are equivalent to the *wu* or shamans of the village. Since so many of the questions put to the oracle concerned political and

45 Bronze pole finial decorated with a human face, a *t'ao t'ieh* mask and an elephant mask behind. Later Shang period, twelfth to eleventh century BC

military affairs, the augur-priests must have wielded considerable influence in these matters. The government of Shang was to some extent a theocracy.

Shang rule probably extended eastwards across the Central Plain of China to the Shantung region, and westwards to the western end of Honan province. Its influence cannot have passed to the south beyond the Yangtze, or spread far among the nomadic populations lying to the north. Sites at which the coarse grey pottery of the Shang period has been discovered do not extend far beyond the southernmost reach of the Yellow river, or westward beyond its junction with the Wei at the point where the provinces of Shansi, Shensi and Honan join. Of military organization we know nothing beyond a hint at the existence of a royal bodyguard and the practice of securing the help of provincial rulers against others of their number who had to be subjugated.

The life of the Shang population can have differed little in essentials from that of the populous city-states of Bronze Age Mesopotamia. The towns were citadels of a ruling class which enjoyed a monopoly of bronze-craft and consequently of the most efficient weapons – which included the chariot. Metal was little used for tools and not at all for agricultural implements. The peasants' equipment had not advanced beyond the Neolithic level; their stone reaping-knives were to persist in use until they were replaced by iron sickles half a millennium later. The fields were tilled with the digging stick and wooden spade. In the towns bronze was the material of chariot-fitments (less as structural parts than for display), of ritual vessels and other appurtenances of the official rites. As in Mesopotamia, these objects were buried with their owners, presumably for their use in a life beyond the grave, although no explicit ideas on this subject can be gleaned from the oracle sentences.

Ill. 45

The idea of the existence of a close-knit political state is probably an invention of later times. The direct rule of the king can have reached only a short distance from his city walls. Beyond, an outer zone of peasant villages might be subject to overlords appointed by the king (the evidence for the beginnings of a feudal system seems to belong to the very end of the Shang rule), and farther still was an ill-defined area in which Shang rulers had from time to time to dispute their suzerainty with other powers.

One such power, established along the river valleys and on the uplands of Shansi and Shensi, was that of the Chou chiefs. It was their attack on Great Shang in 1027 BC that overthrew the corrupt Chao, last of the Shang kings, and founded a new dynasty.

The traditional view of Chinese historians is that the Chou rulers were primitive barbarians who were civilized by inheriting the culture of the Shang people. But it is improbable that the river valleys and highlands which were the homes of the Chou confederacy before their eastward move stood on a much lower cultural level at the time of the conquest than the Shang state itself. It is interesting that the oracle sentences contain no hint of an attack by Chou on Shang, but suggest on the contrary that the Shang ruler provoked attacks on Chou by other tribes, or at other times conferred the title of marquis on the Chou ruler and accepted him as a subordinate.

There are records in history and in the inscriptions cast on bronze vessels of Chou campaigns as far as the eastern seaboard. It seems that garrisons were established throughout the country under loyal commanders who in the first instance were the close associates of the Chou kings. Some hundreds of small city-states were founded, all acknowledging the suzerainty of Chou in a form of feudal hierarchy. The residence remained, however, at Tsung Chou in Shensi until 771 B C, when it was moved to a pre-existing Chou city near the modern Loyang. Around the new capital lay the small state directly governed by the Chou king. By now the great underlords and rulers of provinces had coalesced into some twelve major states whose allegiance to Chou was little more than formal. The king at the centre was only one factor in an uneasy balance of power. He had the duty of performing the national sacrifices to heaven and earth: his rôle as source of honours and material rewards for services rendered by feudal lords and ministers is commemorated in thousands of inscriptions made by the recipients on bronze vessels which were eventually deposited in their graves. Increasingly, the great feudal states engaged in internecine war.

Ill. 49

In the western uplands of the Chou homeland horse-raising had been important probably even in Shang times. In the ninth century a Chou noble is recorded as receiving 600 horses from the Jung barbarians of the north-west. It is of interest to find that the decoration of some bronzes found in the burials of chariots at Anyang, although apparently dating to the end of the Shang period, is more akin to the art of the Chou as it appears in the late eleventh and tenth centuries. In these chariot graves too are found

the animal-headed knives and an unexplained bow-shaped object (interpreted tentatively as a shield mount) which can be paralleled in the Bronze Age finds of the Minusinsk basin in south Siberia. Conversely, the graves of corresponding date in Minusinsk contain for the first time skulls of pronounced Chinese type. It is perhaps not surprising that the horse-raisers of north-west China should have been in touch with tribes of similar livelihood in Siberia, even across the Gobi desert. The charioteers of the Shang

Ills. 46, 47 must have been recruited with their horses from the western provinces, and consequently display features in their equipment which have Chou rather than Shang affinities. The date of the Shang chariot graves, of the bronze parallels with south Siberia and of the appearance there of the Sinoid skulls need not be earlier than the twelfth or eleventh century BC. The comparatively rare socketed axes found at Anyang also resemble closely axes from Minusinsk, although their decoration with Shang-

Ill. 40 style animal masks proves that they were made in Honan. In their Shensi river valleys the Chou tribes could benefit by cultural borrowing both from Central China and from south Siberia.

How far the inhabitants of north-west China at the time of the Chou conquest differed racially from the population of the Central Plain is quite uncertain. The theory that they were of the stock from which descended the Turkish people of later times is supported to some extent by

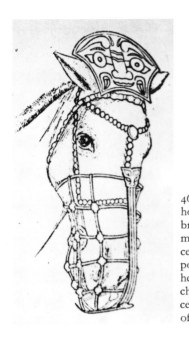

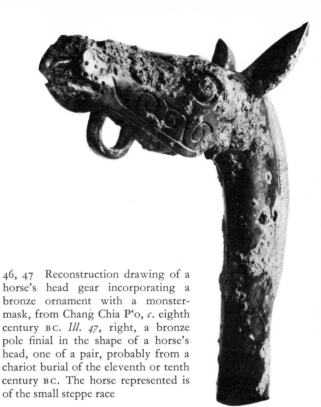

46, 47 Reconstruction drawing of a horse's head gear incorporating a bronze ornament with a monster-mask, from Chang Chia P'o, *c.* eighth century BC. *Ill. 47*, right, a bronze pole finial in the shape of a horse's head, one of a pair, probably from a chariot burial of the eleventh or tenth century BC. The horse represented is of the small steppe race

historical tradition. Arguments based on nomenclature connect them with the supposed ancestors of the Hunnish tribes which appear in the fuller light of history from the second century BC onwards. The attacks by barbarians on the northern frontier were probably caused as much by the expropriation of nomadic tribesmen by the expanding Chinese agricultural community as by organized invasion from without, at least in the earlier centuries of the Chou period. True steppe nomadism, the life of horse-raising, tent-dwelling tribes, despisers of tillage and harriers of the settled peasants within the area of Chinese control (eventually within the line of the Great Wall), seems not to have arisen until late in the history of Chinese expansion to the north and north-west, in the fifth to fourth century BC. Thereafter the attacks of the nomads caused unceasing trouble and expense to the Chinese.

Ills. 50, 51

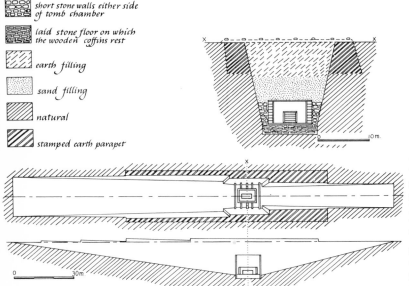

short stone walls either side of tomb chamber

laid stone floor on which the wooden coffins rest

earth filling

sand filling

natural

stamped earth parapet

48 A shaft-tomb with double ramps at Ku Wei Ts'un, near Hui Hsien, Honan province. The burial chamber and coffin are shown in plan and elevation. Late fifth or fourth century BC

The Dissolution of the Feudal State

The state religion of Chou times centred on sacrifice to heaven and earth. Its chief instruments were still the bronze vessels in which meats and wine were offered to cosmic and ancestral spirits. The supreme deity was 'heaven' – T'ien – a more abstract conception than the Shang Ti of Shang times, and one related, according to some, to the heaven-worship of the ancient Turks. The royal succession was now regularly from father to son. A vast ceremonial was elaborated in which the Chou king played the leading rôle and on which the peace of the realm and the abundance of crops were deemed to depend. Books composed in the fourth to third centuries BC, the *Li Chi* and *I Li*, set forth the order of public and private sacrifice and ritual, including the mortification of filial mourning as prescribed by Confucianism, in a loving detail which smacks of the professional ritualist. *Li*, which we translate by 'ritual', though as well as the outward forms it implies a whole philosophy of ordered social

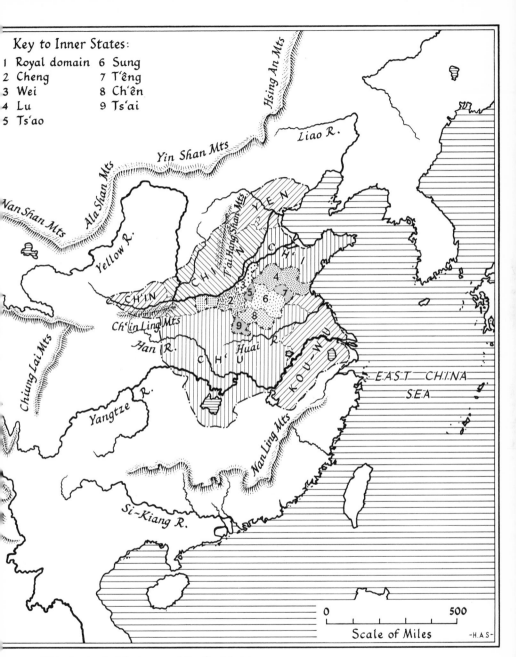

Key to Inner States:

1 Royal domain   6 Sung
2 Cheng   7 T'êng
3 Wei   8 Ch'ên
4 Lu   9 Ts'ai
5 Ts'ao

49   China's physical features and the feudal states

50 The Great Wall of China near the Nanking Gate at Peking. The Wall is a consolidation of stretches of walls originally built in the fourth and third centuries B C against nomads and which were joined and extended by the Ch'in emperor Shih Huang Ti

intercourse and hierarchic submission, was regarded as the principle on which civilization and political well-being rested. Heaven was thought to work in harmony with human affairs, reacting with disasters against mis-behaviour of rulers and subjects, but particularly of the former. The king was such by the mandate of heaven. The royal tombs no longer contained slaughtered victims.

Ill. 48

We now know something too of the spiritual doctrine of the Chou period. After death a man was deemed to have two souls, the *hun* which departed hence and the *po* which lingered by the tomb. The *po* had to be nourished by food offerings, until it gradually faded to nothing. But these concepts, with which in his time Confucius, while not denying their existence, would no more concern himself than with the question of other gods and spirits, received

51   The sentry walk along the top of the Great Wall of China, wide enough to take a horse and cart. The Wall was fourteen hundred miles long and had twenty-five thousand towers. On the left the battlemented wall faced outwards towards the enemy; the inner face had a level top

little attention from the educated class. In royal as in private ritual no priests were employed, the king and the head of the family taking charge of the sacrifices. The religion of sacrifice and *li* was the creed of the Hundred Families – *pai hsing* – as the local rulers came to be called. The commonalty, the 'black-haired people' as the Chou warlords had called them from the start, preserved their old animistic beliefs. In the villages the *wu* still practised his healing and necromantic art, and the spirits of hill and stream had their due offerings.

By the seventh century BC the central Chou state, in theory controller of subordinate states, was reduced to puppet status, and although maintained as a ceremonial head was held ransom to the most powerful state of the day. From the beginning of the seventh century this was Ch'i,

Ill. 49

the state occupying the rich agricultural plains and low hills of Shantung, a centre of trade in salt and in the metal ores which reached it by river from the south. In 704 B C the ruler of Ch'u, a state which embraced a huge territory extending from central Honan to the lake region on the middle Yangtze, had arrogated the title of king – *wang* – in defiance of his theoretical feudal status. The rivalry of Ch'in and Ch'i in the north, the increasing pressure of Ch'u from the south, the varying alignments of the smaller states, including Chou, as they sought protective alliances with different major powers, barbarian inroads such as that of 660 B C when nomads devastated the north Honan state of Wei constitute the characteristic political order and disorder of the whole of the later Chou period.

With the rise of Ch'u begins the incorporation of the south into Chinese culture, accompanying the spread of irrigation farming and bronze technology among peoples just emerging from a tribal hunting economy. In the period aptly called by Chinese historians 'The Warring States' (403–221 B C) the internecine warfare grew still more intensive. A new factor was the aggression of the western hill-state of Ch'in against the central states. This led to the unification of the empire in 221 B C under the Ch'in emperor Shih Huang Ti. When this emperor built *Ills. 50, 51* his famous Great Wall he was joining stretches of pre-existing walls constructed in the fourth and third centuries B C against the nomad attacks which the unsettled state of China now attracted. Throughout these centuries tens of thousands of soldiers (if not the hundreds of thousands spoken of in the histories) were engaged in single battles.

The states could exploit their manpower on an unprecedented scale, as in constructing the canal dug in the fifth century B C to link the basin of the lower Yangtze with that of the Yellow river, or later in the building of the Great Wall. The transport, storage and distribution of grain to the dense population crowding the valleys, which was constantly exposed to flood and famine, was already an important factor in political control. For all this vast coercion of the population by the warring lords, no regular slave system was instituted comparable to that of Italy in the early centuries of the Roman empire. In the domination of unarmed and pacific peasants it was unnecessary. Such slavery as existed was domestic, in the form which survived until recent times. Even under the Shang dynasts, despite the description of that period by present-day Chinese historians as a slave-state, there is no evidence that slave-holding was an essential feature of government or agriculture.

In these troubled times lived Confucius, whose philosophy is a system of ethics for a ruling class, formulated from ideas current in his day. To metaphysics and logic he was indifferent. Moral integrity, loyalty, and fearless advocacy of just and selfless rule are the distinctive characteristics of the Chüntzŭ, the 'superior man'. Confucius' *Tao*, or Way, a rational cosmic order with which rulers and subjects must passively conform in the interest of peace and welfare, is akin to the old conception of a heaven reacting to human affairs. It is enough for the ruler to attune himself to it, and take no active measures, for political order to be restored. Such harmony with the principle can only be achieved by minute attention to the rites and ceremonies collectively designated *Li*. Confucius reasserted an ancient feudal morality against the opportunism and turbulence of the rulers of his day.

Mencius (*c.* 372–289 BC), like Confucius a spokesman for the literati of east China, developed the Confucian philosophy towards à less exclusive humanism. He introduced the notion of 'human-heartedness' as ideally governing social relations, and stated more explicitly that the will of heaven in the choice of a successor to the Chou paramount kingship would be declared through the voice of the 'people', *i.e.* of the ruling class and their clients, the

52　A detail from a tomb wall painting at T'ung-kou, Manchuria, of the fifth to sixth centuries AD shows the typical composite bow in use. Bows used in East Asia have generally been of this kind

literati and landowners. He comes near to recognizing the principle asserted by later Confucian apologists of China's dynastic revolutions, that subjects have a right, even a duty, to rebel against a corrupt ruler. The theory of the command of heaven investing a king is very different from the divine right of European monarchs.

In Motzŭ (c. 479–381 BC) we find a determined opponent of the Confucian idea: for him family affection must be extended to all mankind – universal love and pacifism are proposed as the cures for the ills of the times. At about the same period is said to have lived Lao-Tzŭ, whose philosophy urges man to surrender his will to the cosmic process of the Tao, in a spirit far removed from the positive ethic of Confucius. The quietist and anti-rational tenor of his philosophy has attracted an interest in the

53-55   One of the main weapons in China, even after the introduction of the sword in the sixth century BC, was the halberd, *ko*. *Ills. 53* and *55* are examples of jade ritual halberd blades with bronze sockets which have *t'ao t'ieh* masks on them. *Ill. 54*, centre, is entirely of bronze

West in recent times almost comparable to that which Confucian concepts held for the French *philosophes* of the eighteenth century.

Weapons

Besides bronze and pottery vessels the tombs of Shang and Chou have preserved large numbers of weapons. Those of the Shang period are surprising for their small range of types and their relative simplicity. Chief among them are the bow and the halberd. No example of the former has survived, but its shape may be judged from its appearance in some of the emblematic characters cast on bronze vessels. There it can be seen to have a double curve, with the upper tip turning strongly inwards. Its length cannot have been much less than 1·25 metres. The shape is virtual proof that the bow was of the compound type, as favoured by the Asian mounted warriors of later and historical times: a bow built of several, possibly many pieces, and possibly of a mixture of wood, bone and horn. The double curve provides great power for a

Ill. 52

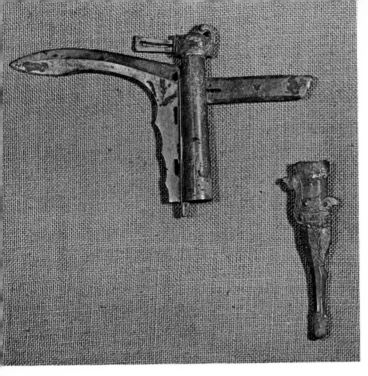

56 Bronze halberd, *ko*, with the hafting finial and ferrule which survived with it. This is one of the few specimens of which all the bronze parts of a halberd have been preserved together. It was found near Shou Hsien, Anhui province. Fourth to third century BC

comparatively short pull, and makes the bow specially suitable for shooting from horseback or from the confined space of the box of a chariot. As far as is known at present, horses were not ridden in Shang times, but the chariot was important in warfare. Shang arrowheads were made of bone and bronze, usually double-bladed with a short tang, or (in bone) as faceted or tapering points. The bronze arrowheads, with their bone copies, first appear in Shang II, on the site at Erh Li Kang. Later in the Shang period forms with curving edges, pierced blades and barbs of exaggerated length were made. There was little variation in the form of the arrowheads until about 400 BC, when an important change took place, to be noticed below.

Ills. 53, 55

The other important Shang weapon was the halberd called *ko*. It is a form of weapon peculiar to China, without even approximate parallels in other countries of the Far East. It has been compared to certain long-bladed axes of Early Bronze Age date found in south Siberia, but the resemblance is not close, and no cultural connexion

57, 58 A bronze blade, possibly for mounting on a haft, of the Shang period. The back of the blade is perforated by T-shaped notches. The band of decoration, showing five ram-heads, has a spiral ground of typical Shang pattern. *Ill. 58*, right, a jade knife, with three perforations along the back and incised ornament not all of which is original. Shang or Early Chou dynasty

can be established to account for any borrowing and adaptation. Nor does the *ko* derive very plausibly from a form of stone axe found in Neolithic China, as has been argued. The halberd consists of a blade 15 to 25 cms long, and up to 5 cms wide, usually very slightly curving, furnished with a flat tang a few inches long which passed through the shaft to which the blade lay at right angles. The end of the tang, which was thus visible, is often decorated with a monster-mask, in rare instances inlaid with turquoise. At the root of the blade is a transverse guard which lay along the shaft. In the later development of the *ko*, through the whole of the Chou period, the blade increased its curvature, the tang projected farther and the guard, forming a heel to the blade, extended farther back along the shaft. Rare examples, of the fourth to third centuries B C, were furnished with a tubular mount strengthening the haft around the slot through which the tang passed. Already in Shang times the *ko* shaft had a bronze ferrule (triple-spiked) at its lower

Ill. 56

end, and the ferrules of late Chou times (single-spiked) assumed a schematic bird shape and often bore rich ornaments, cast or inlaid. In the Shang period the length of the *ko* shaft was about a metre, so that the weapon could be brandished like a battle-axe, but later it extended to some 1·5 metres, and the weapon must have functioned more like a pike or halberd. At this later stage the *ko* was sometimes completed with a spearhead projecting a short distance above the halberd blade.

Ill. 57

Ill. 59

Another form of halberd, found only in the Shang or early Chou period, consisted of a long narrow blade placed parallel to the haft and generally curving a little on its end. The great axes, often elaborately and grotesquely decorated with relief and open work, which were recovered from the larger Shang tombs, served to behead the funeral victims: in the emblems cast on vessels a similar axe is sometimes shown poised over the headless trunk of a man. Similar axes no doubt were used in warfare. Shang spearheads were of laurel-leaf outline, not dissimilar from those made in the West, but the treatment of the tail of the blade is individual. On either side of the tube of the hafting socket the edges of the blade run down and expand a little giving a concave curve, and are then finished in a straight line in fish-tail shape. Perforations in these flanges served for thongs which anchored the spearhead to its haft.

From the later part of the Shang dynasty and in the early centuries of the Chou period we must suppose, however, that the chariot was the determining factor in warfare. It was used, as in Greece and the Near East, mainly to convey soldiers who dismounted to fight. Over the Central Plain, where paths were quickly made, the mobility of the chariotry gave the Chinese decisive superiority over their chariotless enemies. In the eighth century it is recorded that the forces of the state of Ch'eng fought with chariots against the foot-soldiers of the Jung

59 Bronze ritual axe, *yüeh*, of the kind used for beheading human funeral victims. Shang dynasty, twelfth or eleventh century BC

tribes. The Shang chariot was constructed in all essential parts of wood: a simple rectangular frame carried, above, the floor of the box, measuring only about 1·25 × 0·91 metres, and, beneath, the axle-beam and the shaft engaging in it at the centre. A yoke-beam rested on the necks of the two shaft-horses, which exerted their pull on traces attached to the chariot in the region of the driver's box. If the strain was taken on neck-bands, as in the classical chariot of the Near East, the horses must have tended to choke themselves and their effort was reduced accordingly: hence sometimes the necessity of the outer pair of trace-horses – four horses in all to draw the comparatively light load of two soldiers and their weapons. The wheel rims were of wood, bound with perishable material, and encircling slender spokes. On the site of the city of Shang at Hsiao T'un five burials of chariots were excavated in the open area which was bounded on three sides by buildings. Here the burial of the charioteers and the horses at the side of the vehicle could be observed, and some bronzes (notably arrowheads and knives with horse-head pommels) were recovered; but none of these tombs provided such clear evidence of the structure of the chariot as important as the chariot grave excavated at Ta Ssǔ K'ung near Anyang. The other burials at the place

Ill. 62

Ill. 60

were of the smaller Shang kind, with bodies laid singly and prone, accompanied by pottery vessels and a few bronze arrowheads. There was no sign of a tomb of royal dimensions. In the chariot tomb the forms of some of the timbers had been preserved by a process which has been encountered in Chinese excavations several times in recent years, and is not unknown elsewhere. As the wood, surrounded by compact earth, rotted away, it was replaced by a fine dust which eventually turned into a firm mass distinct in texture from the encasing earth and capable of being separated from it by careful excavation. Traces thus preserved were positive mouldings of the chariot parts. In the case of the Ta Ssǔ K'ung chariot the possibility of recovering the exact forms of the chariot through observing the soil trace was not fully realized by the excavators, or perhaps the disturbed state of the soil had obscured the margins of the soil cast. The chariot had been buried fully assembled, channels being dug to accommodate the wheels and main members of the frame, so that the bottom of the charioteer's box lay on the floor of the pit. The method of attaching the axle to the main beam cannot be deduced. There was no trace of bronze at this place, so that this juncture can only have been assembled by wooden pins and lashing of rope or thongs. The after-end of the main beam had a slight twist to the right, no doubt fortuitous. The length of the axle between the hubs is about 1·8 metres, the overall length 3 metres. The spokes of one wheel (of 1·46 metres diameter) were clearly preserved by the earth cast, and numbered eighteen. Bronze axle caps remained in place, and rows of bronze discs seem to mark the line of leather traces to which they were originally attached. Over each horse's neck was placed a V-shaped yoke, made of wood now vanished, protected on the upper side by bronze sheathing. The two horses, dead when buried, had been laid symmetrically on their sides with their backs towards the beam. The

Ill. 60

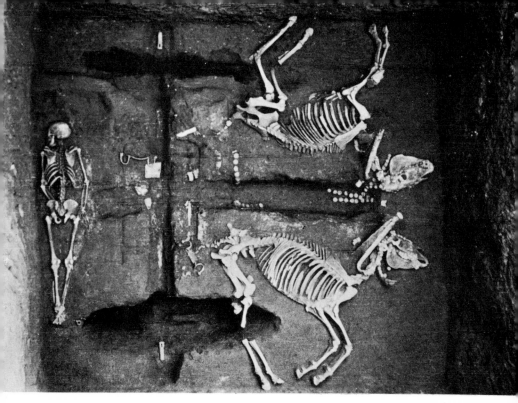

60 Burial of a chariot with horses and charioteer at Ta Ssǔ K'ung Ts'un, near Anyang, Honan province. Parts of the pit floor were dug away to accommodate the lower part of the wheels, the axle and the shaft. The charioteer lies prone behind the chariot. Shang dynasty, eleventh century BC

charioteer's box surprises by its small size, being on a foundation only about a metre × 80 cms, as can be measured from the soil trace. The actual floor cannot have been much bigger – one would expect the wheels to be allowed good clearance – and only sufficient for warrior and driver to stand together when the chariot was in motion, certainly not spacious enough for the two men to fight from the vantage of their vehicle. In and near the box were strewn various bronzes: a knife, arrowheads, and two bow-shaped objects. The last are of uncertain purpose: they clearly relate to the occupants' armament (shield or bow mounts?) rather than the fittings of the chariot. The bronze bell which seems to have been slung beneath the box is a fanciful addition: it is hardly large enough to awe enemies or hearten friends. The chariot pits at Hsiao T'un each contained two men, presumably the warrior and his driver, but here only the driver has accompanied his vehicle. Two horses were the usual complement, but one Hsiao T'un grave held four, the trace-horses (like the Homeric *paraseiroi*) as well as the main couple.

Ills. 79, 80
Ill. 61

In the Chou period the most informative burials of chariots are those excavated at Shang Ts'un Ling and Liu Li Ko (Hui Hsien), both in Honan province, dated respectively to the eighth–seventh and the fourth–third centuries BC. The structure of the vehicle has changed little from the Shang type. Of the eleven buried at Shang Ts'un Ling, five were preserved virtually intact in the earth cast. The main beams were made to curve above the level of the box floor, which remained level, and at the ends of the beams the trace of the cross-bar bearing the yokes was preserved. The base of the box measured 90 × 130 cms, the wheel diameter was 125 cms with a rim 7 × 7 cms in section and had 25 fine, tapering spokes. The wheel-hubs measured 35 cms in length, and turned on an axle 7·5 cms in diameter. They must have been built by pegging and lashing, for no bronze parts were preserved. The dimensions indicate a slender construction which well attests the firm and accurate carpentry of the time. The great length of the hub is required to minimize the pressure and friction of wood turning on wood, lubricated by animal fat or pitch. The sides of the boxes were formed of vertical and horizontal withies, widely spaced and attached (*i.e.* not intertwined) at their intersections.

Ills. 62, 63

The Liu Li Ko pit contained no less than nineteen uncoupled chariots, closely packed in two rows, with the beam of each vehicle resting on the box of the one in front. The horses had been buried in an adjoining pit. The chariots are essentially similar to those of Shang Ts'un

61 Chariot burials with horses at Shang Ts'un Ling, Honan province. The earth cast has preserved the shape of the chariots virtually intact in five out of the eleven chariots found. Chou dynasty, eighth to seventh centuries BC

Ling, with 26-spoked wheels and similarly proportioned rims and hubs. The rails of the boxes had been coated with lacquer paint. Some of the wheels were made to give a slightly conical profile, the rims advanced outwards beyond the plane in which the spokes entered the hub, and two parallel struts joined the rims near the diameter. This 'dishing' allowed a greater width to the box. The harness was still effected by yokes, and possibly the effect inferred above for the Shang harness had not yet been eliminated. Harness was indeed not improved upon until Han times, when a form taking the draught from the horse's chest was adopted. This invention anticipated the European device of a hard collar by many centuries, and the improvement it gave to locomotion was very great.

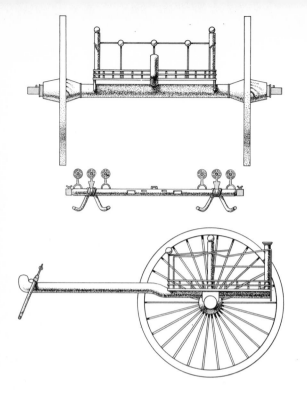

62, 63 A reconstruction of a chariot from Liu Li Ko of the type illustrated *in situ* opposite in *Ill. 63*. This tomb was found in 1950 and contained nineteen chariots buried in two rows, each chariot with its shaft resting on the box of the one in front. All bronze fittings were removed prior to the burial of the chariots. The structure of the wooden parts had left traces in the earth and was recovered by careful excavation

The Early Iron Age

The exact date of the first use of iron in China, the place of its discovery, or the source of knowledge of iron if we suppose it to have been introduced from abroad, are still obscure questions. Literary evidence argues a rather earlier date than the present archaeological evidence, unsupported, seems to warrant. Allusions to iron in early writings point to a knowledge of it in the seventh or sixth century B C. The *Tso Chuan* supplies the earliest closely datable reference when it speaks of the casting of iron cauldrons in a year corresponding to 512 B C. Penal laws were inscribed on these vessels, which had been made from iron levied from the people by a minister of the state of Ch'in. If the evidence of this text is accepted, we must assume that iron was common and that casting technique was well advanced by the end of the sixth century. Archaeological evidence, however, points to the earliest casting only about 400 B C. Even so it is this early

practice of casting which astonishes the Western historian. In Europe this technique was not known until the fourteenth century AD. The forging of iron, a much simpler process, one step beyond the smelting of the ore itself, might be expected to precede casting in China by a large margin, as it did in Europe. But while the relation of the two processes cannot yet be fully elucidated historically in China, it seems certain that no considerable period of forging alone preceded casting. Rather, the reverse seems to be true, the evidence for casting falling a little later. The continued use of bronze alongside iron, the nobler metal serving still for swords and halberds and the ornamental chariot axle-caps, echoes the parallel situation in the West. But, to the glory of the later craft of China, bronze-work did not suffer the eclipse which descended on it in many parts of Europe once iron was plentiful.

It is less remarkable perhaps that one of the earliest uses of iron in China was the manufacture of agricultural tools,

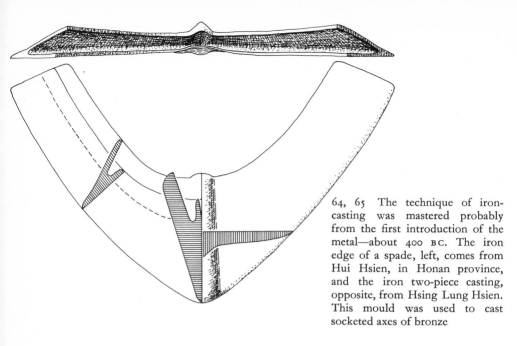

64, 65 The technique of iron-casting was mastered probably from the first introduction of the metal—about 400 BC. The iron edge of a spade, left, comes from Hui Hsien, in Honan province, and the iron two-piece casting, opposite, from Hsing Lung Hsien. This mould was used to cast socketed axes of bronze

Ill. 64

Ill. 65

such as those found in a tomb of the fourth century BC at Hui Hsien in Honan. These included the cutting edges for squared and pointed wooden spades, and some narrow spades made wholly of the metal. We need not, however, think of these digging tools replacing the stone and wooden hoes of the ordinary farmer. It was an ancient custom to bury in a great tomb some of the implements used in excavating it, or miniature symbolic versions of them. No doubt stone hoes continued in use even in the Central Plain until Han times, and in the less civilized parts of China – particularly the southern hilly regions – until very much later. At Hsing Lung in Jehol province eighty-seven iron moulds for spades, chisels, chariot parts, etc., were recovered from the site of a foundry. The forms indicate a date not later than the fourth century BC, and it appears that iron moulds were used in casting bronze.

No swords, and not even satisfactory daggers, appear among the weapons buried in Shang tombs. Short bronze swords, some of them tanged for hafting, but mostly having a grip cast on, appear towards the end of the sixth century BC. At first they are little more than dirks. The

typical sword of the fourth century is little different from
the *akinakes* of the steppe nomads, to whom it probably
owes its introduction into China. It seldom exceeds 75
cms in length, and has a cast ribbed handle which was
bound with cord. The slight, sudden narrowing of the
profile about one-third of the length from the points, as
seen in many of the blades, recalls the 'carp's tongue'
finesse which is a feature of some Late Bronze Age swords
in Europe.

In the later third century a new type of sword appeared,
apparently an enlarged version of a knife-shape also of
north-western, nomad origin. The blade is single-edged,
barely tapered, and terminates at the handle in an oval
ring. These swords were made both of bronze and iron,
and the longest of them exceed 1·25 metres. Double-edged
blades with tangs for hafting and of equal length are also
known in both metals, and apparently are contemporary
with the single-edged kind. But bronze versions of the
new long sword are rare; they copy the iron sword in size,
but naturally they could not equal it in toughness or in
hardness and thinness of the cutting edge.

Ill. 68

Ills. 67, 69

Ill. 66

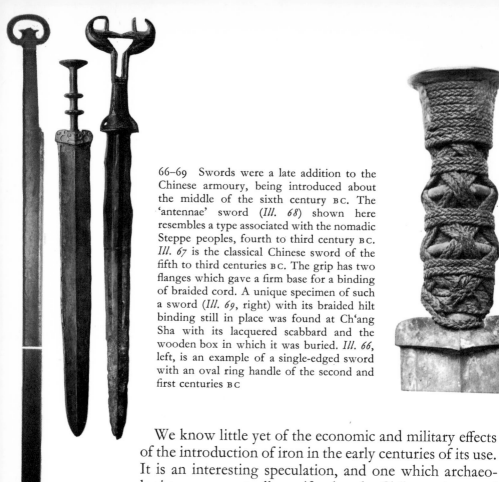

66–69 Swords were a late addition to the Chinese armoury, being introduced about the middle of the sixth century B C. The 'antennae' sword (*Ill. 68*) shown here resembles a type associated with the nomadic Steppe peoples, fourth to third century B C. *Ill. 67* is the classical Chinese sword of the fifth to third centuries B C. The grip has two flanges which gave a firm base for a binding of braided cord. A unique specimen of such a sword (*Ill. 69*, right) with its braided hilt binding still in place was found at Ch'ang Sha with its lacquered scabbard and the wooden box in which it was buried. *Ill. 66*, left, is an example of a single-edged sword with an oval ring handle of the second and first centuries B C

Ill. 70

We know little yet of the economic and military effects of the introduction of iron in the early centuries of its use. It is an interesting speculation, and one which archaeologists may eventually verify, that the Ch'in armies owed their decisive might to their monopoly of the long iron swords. Shih Huang Ti is said to have melted down the bronze arms taken from his enemies to make ten human images; if his troops were armed with the iron sword, the shorter bronze sword would be of no use to them. Certainly after the unification, and in Han times, the chief weapons were regularly made of iron. An exception is the cross-bow lock, whose intricate mechanism could still be cast only in bronze. Its invention probably soon after 200 B C marks the last important advance in armament before the production of firearms. The cross-bow was as important in the stabilization of the north-west frontier as the Wall itself.

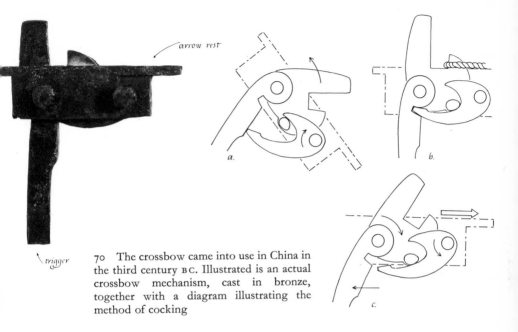

arrow rest

trigger

70 The crossbow came into use in China in the third century BC. Illustrated is an actual crossbow mechanism, cast in bronze, together with a diagram illustrating the method of cocking

In the wars of the last two centuries of the Chou feudal period, when even the forms of feudal subordination were ignored, large infantry armies took the field. The fighting chariot can hardly have played any significant part in the battles. As China became increasingly embroiled in inter-necine war the nomads inhabiting Mongolia began to harry the northern marches with cavalry, and the Chinese had set against them horsemen of their own. But even frontier defence was based mainly on infantry. The nomads shot with the compound bow from the saddle, but foot-soldiers manning the Great Wall, armed with powerful cross-bows, could shoot farther and more accurately. Under Shih Huang Ti of Ch'in the line of the Great Wall was completed, taking in long sections built in earlier times. Its defence was elaborately organized by the Han emperors, eventually reaching a length of fourteen hundred miles and incorporating twenty-five thousand towers.

Ills. 50, 51

CHAPTER FIVE

The Artistic Tradition of
the Shang and Chou

Bronze vessels

The art of the Shang and Chou periods finds its fullest expression in the bronze vessels. They are hardly to be matched for beauty of form and decoration and skill of execution at any other time or place in the ancient world. The shapes of the vessels were no doubt derived in the first place from the pottery vessels. The *ting* and *li* descend from the characteristic pottery shapes of the north-eastern Neolithic, while the *kuei*, which became the commonest form after the Chou conquest, copies a shape found in the grey pottery of the Central Plain. But shapes such as the *chüeh*, *chia* and *kuang*, specially characteristic of the Shang, are difficult to imagine in any material but bronze. In proportions and profile the best vessels show a command of plastic effect which raises them to the level of great art. The ornament is adapted to the most elaborate forms with consummate skill, enriching the surface and enhancing the relief. Yet the vessels were repetitious craft products, in which stock ornamental motifs appear in but a few combinations and variation of shape was permitted only within narrow limits. Nevertheless, in the Shang period and in the earliest decades of the Chou dynasty the finest pieces show a feeling for form, rooted in but transcending utility, which can be compared with the porcelains of the Sung period. The skill displayed in adapting animal shapes

Ill. 71

Ills. 72, 75

Ills. 73, 74

Ill. 76

71, 72 The three-legged bronze ritual vessel right, a *ting*, was used for the preparation of sacrificial food. Below, a *kuei*, for holding cooked food, is decorated with stylized elephants confronted on either side of the handle to make a design similar to the *t'ao t'ieh* mask. An inscription on the interior of the bowl in early Chou script refers to a gift of land to the Marquis of Hsing

89

73–76 Above are two examples of vessels (*chia*) for warming the black millet wine, of the early and later Shang dynasty respectively. The ritual bronze food vessel, *kuei*, below, was cast, according to its inscription, for a Marquis of K'ang to commemorate his receipt of a royal brevet enfeoffing him in the land of Mei following a revolt by the heir of the last Shang ruler. It can thus be dated to the end of the eleventh dynasty. *Ill. 76*, opposite, is a *tsun*, a bronze ritual vessel cast in the shape of two rams

77　A bronze frontal of the type as worn by horses (*cf. Ill. 46*) decorated with an animal mask. Early Chou dynasty, tenth to seventh century BC

to the requirements of a vessel and to the resources of ornament is repeated in the neat adaptation of ornament to ritual axes and knives, weapons and the decorative plaques which were fixed in the dashboards of chariots.

From the start the level of skill in bronze casting compares with that of the high Bronze Age of the Mediterranean civilizations. The employment of the *cire-perdue* method has been suspected but not proved, while it is certain, on the other hand, that direct casting in pottery piece-moulds was practised. The rendering of detail is astonishingly fine and free from blemish. The bronze alloy differs from that of most of the rest of the Bronze Age world in the greatly varying quantity of tin which it contains. The difficulty of bringing the ore from its source in the central and southern hills may be the cause, but even at a later period, when this region was fully controlled, the ingredients of the metal are not constant. On the other hand, the large proportion of lead included in the bronze, particularly in that of Shang date, must be a deliberate addition. By helping the flow of the molten metal and preventing gas bubbles it improved the rendering of detailed ornament. Its effect on colour was to reduce the metallic brilliance of the reddish surface: for we must picture the vessels in their original state without the beautiful green and blue patination which they have acquired in the soil and for which they are so much prized by Western collectors. Chinese collectors always favoured a dark surface, and rubbed on grease to achieve it. In China the ancient vessels were treasured, to our knowledge, from Han times onwards, chiefly for their august associations as ritual vessels and for the inscriptions many of them carry.

Ills. 72, 75

92

78 Gold openwork dagger handle of the Chou dynasty, *c.* 400 BC, a unique piece. Gold of any kind of this date is rare. The decoration is an interlaced pattern of dragons of a quality surpassing even that produced on the bronzes of the period

79, 80 Bronze chariot pole fittings inlaid with gold and silver. The bull's head, above, is unparalleled in naturalistic animal art of the late Chou dynasty. Below, the mounts are in the shape of mythical animals. The fittings were found at Chin Ts'un, Honan province, not far from Lolang, the Chou dynasty capital

81 Bronze ritual food container (*fang-yi*) of the Shang dynasty. It is highly ornamented with ornate seams, *t'ao t'ieh* masks and bird motifs in the panels at the base

82 Types of bronze sacrificial vessels of the late Shang dynasty, thirteenth to
twelfth century BC. 1, *chüeh*; 2, *chih*; 3, *tsun*; 4, *li*; 5, *yü*; 6, *tsun*; 7, *hsien*; 8, *p'an*;
9, *yü*; 10, *ting*; 11, *p'ou*; 12, *kuei*. Nos 1, 2, 3, 5 and 6 are for wine; 8 for water,
and the remainder for food

Ills. 82, 83

It was a traditional belief in China that the various
shapes of the earliest bronze vessels – those of the Shang
and the earlier Chou dynasty – were appropriated to particular sacrifices. The ritualist literature compiled in the
third–second centuries BC (but containing much earlier
matter) recorded minute regulations in the use made of
each vessel. Many vessel names survived in the ancient
literature, and assumptions were evidently made as to·
which vessel type a name denoted. This ritual study was
revived with the use of systematic antiquarianisms in the
eleventh–twelfth centuries, and the vessels were classified
by name and dynasty, being allotted to the Shang, Chou
or Han period. The names by which the vessels are
designated today are in the main those employed by the
Sung antiquarians. In some cases the inscription cast on a
vessel, by naming it, confirms the traditional term applied
to it. In other cases the traditional name seems to be con-
tradicted, and altogether the impression is gained that the

83 It is very rarely that so large a set of bronze ritual vessels is found together. The example shown is of early Chou dynasty date of the late eleventh or the early tenth century BC, and came from a tomb at Feng Hsiang, Shensi province, in 1901. Each vessel had its prescribed and specific use. Several may be identified by reference to the illustration of types opposite

use of the vessel names in ancient times was by no means subject to the strict regulation which the ritualist writers would have us believe.

The vessels as a whole may be classified according to the contents they were destined to receive (as judged from the indications of inscriptions and from the oldest ritual literature):

Food vessels:	for preparing the food:	Ting, Li, Hsien.	*Ill. 71*
	for holding the food:	Tui, Fu.	*Ills. 84, 85*
Wine vessels:	for holding the wine:	Yi, Yü, Tsun,	*Ills. 86-88*
		Hu, Lei, Kuang.	*Ills. 93, 95*
	for drinking the wine:	Chüeh, Ku.	*Ill. 89*
Water vessels:	for holding the water:	P'an.	
	for pouring the water:	Ho, Yi	*Ill. 90*
		(a different word from the Yi above).	

84, 85 The ritual food vessel, *tui*, above, has a bowl and a reversible covering which are almost identical in shape. It was found at Pao-chi, Shensi province and is of late Chou dynasty date, probably fifth century BC. Below, a double food vessel (*fu*) for cooked food is of the Eastern Chou dynasty

86–88 Three examples of the deep bucket-shaped bronze vessel, *yü*, for holding wine, all of which are of the Shang dynasty. All are highly ornamented in typical Shang style, the example below left representing a tiger-monster devouring or protecting a boy who has pierced ears. A prominent *t'ao t'ieh* mask decorates the belly of the *yü* below right and a band of *kuei* dragons above and below it

89 A tall slender bronze goblet for drinking wine, *ku*, of the Shang dynasty. A *t'ao t'ieh* decorates the centre of the stem divided by a flange

The primitive motive of the sacrifice was no doubt, as in other times and countries, to attract and conciliate gods and spirits, including ancestral spirits. Eventually the vessels became symbols of the feudal order, being cast by persons who had received praise and various gifts – often including metal for the casting of the vessel – from their feudal superiors. The vessels were destined, according to inscriptions appearing on many of them, to be used in sacrifice to the recipients' ancestors, and to be 'treasured perpetually' by their descendants. On vessels of Shang date the commonest formula inscribed is brief, naming the person who had the vessel cast, indicating the ancestor by a ritual title (a symbol for one day of the ten-day calendar cycle when the sacrifice is presumed to have been performed) and ending merely with *tsun yi*, vessel for

90 A bronze ritual vessel for pouring wine, *ho*. The lid is in the form of a human face with large ears, and *kuei* dragons with large claws decorate the body on either side of the spout

91–93 Above, a bronze ritual water vessel, *yi*. The handle is modelled as a bull head and deformed bird figures decorate the surface above the body fluting. *Ill. 92*, left, is a bronze *chih*, a tall cup for drinking wine of which this is a typical example. *Ill. 93*, opposite, is a *hu*, a deep wine container with vertical tubular lugs for holding a rope handle. It is inlaid with malachite

94 Chou dynasty pottery, showing typical forms of the fifth to fourth centuries BC. The painted decoration of the *tou*, above right, is in black, white and red

sacrifice, or *pao tsun yi*, precious vessel for sacrifice. The fuller inscriptions began to appear, with striking suddenness, on vessels cast after the Chou conquest of the Shang realm on the Central Plain. The rulers of the Chou confederacy appear to have been no less literate than the Shang whom they subjected, possibly more so. The traditional theory that they were barbarians who became civilized through contact with the Shang at the moment of the conquest is part of the Confucians' myth of history. The kind of ceremony which bronze vessels were cast to commemorate in the early Chou period is well illustrated from a *ho* (wine jug) of the tenth century BC.

'Third month, first quarter, day *ting hai*, King Mu, being in Hsia Yu, offered the sweet wine, and Ching Po the Great Ritualist responded with the *She* rite: and

95 The strange *kuang*, shaped like a sauce-boat, held wine. The lid of this specimen is decorated with a tiger mask and an owl mask, and a duck-like bird looks out from the back of the lid

King Mu offered the *mieh* rite to Chang Fu. Then (the King) came to Ching Po's place, and Ching Po was great in respect and failed in nothing. Chang Fu performed the *mieh li* rite, and made bold to wish for the great prosperity of the Son of Heaven. To commemorate these occasions he had this sacral vessel made.'

The interest of the vessel shapes declines after the beginning of the Chou period. The basic forms of the *ting* tripod and the *hu* vase continue, and for a time the handled wine vessel called *yü*. The functions of the vessels, chiefly the cooking and presentation of food, the mixing and pouring of wine offerings, remained the same, but their shapes were clearly not so rigorously prescribed as the ritual manuals of the fourth–third centuries would have us believe.

Ill. 71
Ill. 93
Ills. 86–88

Ill. 94

Ornament

Ill. 41

The ornament of the Shang period consists principally of the monster-mask called *t'ao t'ieh* (a glutton – so named in later times when it was supposed to symbolize a warning against greed), various forms of dragon, other animals such as cicada, silkworm and birds, and geometric figures. One of the latter, a kind of square spiral resembling a Greek key-fret, forms a continuous pattern, either covering the whole surface and the other motifs, or serving as a background to the main elements. Chance resemblance to an ideograph has earned for it the name *lei wen* – thunder pattern. This art of pattern is essentially linear, and as such foreshadows the predilection for flat, linear form which distinguishes Chinese art as a whole. It is also an animal art inasmuch as it composes, resolves and recombines patterns derived from animal shapes (albeit mythical ones) and combines them with geometric figures. Thus it belongs to the Asiatic tradition known in

Ills. 96–98

later times from the art of the Steppes.

96–98 Nomad art delighted in representations of battles between animals, real or imaginary, and fantastic motifs; and Ordos bronzes of this style, mainly used as harness mounts, were an influence in Han art. The Ordos bronze, opposite, shows horses attacking each other. *Ill. 97*, above, shows a wolf attacking a horse in a forest, and on the gilded plaque, right, two ibexes are shown in the dense foliage of a wood

The relation of the Chinese tradition of animal art to the art of the Steppe nomads, how far China was the recipient or the originator in an exchange of decorative themes, is an obscure problem. Where an early connexion might be sought, between Shang China and the art of the Minusinsk basin in south Siberia, no intimate relationship can be traced. The animal-headed knives of Siberian type found at Anyang fall out of the general artistic context of Shang, and perhaps were imported into Honan from the north-west. Much later, in the second–first century BC, *Ills. 96–98* the animal-style bronze plaques found in the Ordos region of China, and allied influences in Han art, mark a considerable influence of the nomad style from beyond the north-west frontier. Whether in the first instance China contributed to the genesis of the art of the eastern Steppes (as represented, for example, in the fourth-first centuries BC, in the Pazyryk tumuli of the Altai) seems at least doubtful. The influence cannot in any case have been as direct as that of Hellenistic Greece on the art of the Scythians of south Russia.

In the first two or three centuries of the Chou period the motifs of the bronze ornament are broader and simpler than that of Shang; bands of abstract pattern barely betray their derivation from the older dragon figures. Scale patterns and wave-shaped patterns, larger and coarser than eleventh-century designs, come to predominate, and the decoration is sparser. An important change begins about the middle of the seventh century, as seen in the famous groups of vessels from Hsin Cheng in Honan and Li Yü in north Shansi. The vessel shapes are more elaborate, with a new tendency to flamboyance in the outlines; the continuous pattern of the decoration, still based on serpentine dragons, consists of smaller, tighter units, and reveals a new principle of design: interlacery, which had earlier (however much the motifs came near to the idea) been almost meticulously avoided. Influence from a

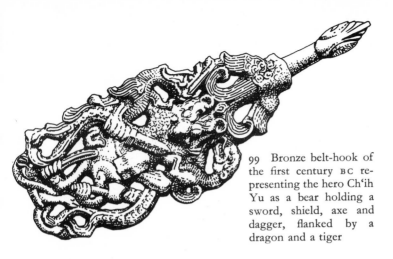

99 Bronze belt-hook of the first century BC representing the hero Ch'ih Yu as a bear holding a sword, shield, axe and dagger, flanked by a dragon and a tiger

Steppe tradition has been invoked to account for this change, but no Steppe material of sufficiently early date can be cited in proof. The continuous repetition of small identical motifs is repugnant to the Steppe styles as we know them later.

Other trends in the bronze decoration arose towards the middle of the sixth century and may have been the result of outside influence. These are the styles associated with the region of the Huai valley and the state of Ch'u. In these the small unit of the ornament has generally a spiralized circular element from which extends a narrow triangle or curled feather. The closely packed repetition of this motif enlivens the surface as never before, and makes demands on the caster's skill beyond even the intricate ornament of the Shang bronzes. The decoration is no longer, as in Shang, the metal version of motifs invented in softer, carved materials, but one created for metal.

From the fifth to the third centuries BC the different styles found cast and inlaid on bronze in gold, silver and turquoise are modifications of the Huai valley style. They appear increasingly in delicately traced figures from which the 'spiral and feather' has vanished but not its dynamic quality. In the third century the pattern is often organized

Ills. 102, 103

100, 101　A bronze figure of a kneeling servant, of the fifth or early fourth century BC. Representations of the human form at this period are comparatively rare. This particular example is typical of the crude style used in such figures. The cylinders were probably intended to hold the stem of a lamp. The back view of the figure shows his hair tied in a chignon and a sheathed sword slung at his waist

in oblong units, which become increasingly symmetrical and heraldic in effect. Towards the end of the last century BC, however, the geometrical and abstract figures, though still present in lacquer and textiles, are yielding ground to a current of naturalism, conventionalized in a spirit that owes something to the nomad tradition. Such naturalism is the most characteristic invention of Han art: lithe tigers are pictured on bronzes in a conventionalized hilly landscape, crouching bears furnish the feet of bronze vessels, horses and a new newt-like dragon are shaped on belt-hooks. Even in the fantasy of interlaced and contorted bodies the animal forms are instinct with new life. In

Ill. 99

102, 103 The lively animal designs on the decorated axe above, are typical of the scrolled style which became established in the southern Ch'u state. The axe dates from the sixth century BC. *Ill. 103*, right, a bronze spearhead inscribed with characters inlaid with gold, with inlaid turquoise at the socket and decorated with variegated colouring of the metal surface. The inscription is in the ornamental 'bird script' in vogue in the southern states of Ch'u and Yüeh in the fifth and fourth centuries BC. The inscription reads 'spear of Chou Shao, King of Yüeh, for his personal use'. The variegation of the bronze surface was a technique practised in the Ch'u area. It is not known how the effect was achieved

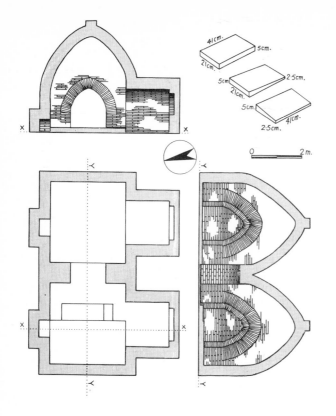

104, 105 A Han dynasty tomb in the eastern suburbs of Canton. The insert, top right, shows the shapes of some of the bricks used. Below, a pottery model boat, ancestor to the modern sampan, from this tomb. The model shows a decked flat-bottomed boat with deck houses like those still in use, roofed with matting and communicating with the 'tween deck space. Forward, there are three holes a side for oars and the steering oar is mounted on the port side, in contrast to the starboard mounting usual in the West

106 Bronze openwork ornament, possibly a harness mount, depicting wolves attacking a deer. It was excavated at Shih Chai Shan, Yünnan. First century BC

some of the pottery statuettes placed in tombs we see the attempt to portray the movements of dancers. In these and in the figures of servants and others, in the portraits *Ills. 100, 101, 105* of officials which decorate the famous painted basket *Ills. 107–109* found at Lolang in Korea, and in the stone bas-reliefs on *Ill. 110* the walls of elaborate underground tombs, the pursuit of naturalism and the abandonment of geometric pattern mark the beginning of a new epoch in Chinese art, the foundation of an artistic bias which has lasted to the present time.

What has been said of the evolution of artistic styles as *Ill. 111* seen in the sacrificial vessels might be illustrated in many

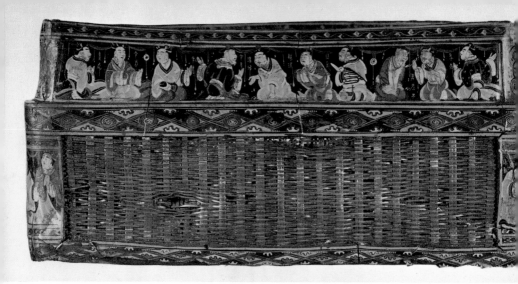

107, 108 A lacquered basket from an early first century AD tomb at Lolang, a Chinese colony in Korea. It shows a marked pursuit of the naturalism of everyday life, typical of early Han art, in the animated conversations between the gentlemen depicted. This is also reflected in the attitude of the players in the game of *liu po*, below. They are of green glazed pottery and come from a tomb of the first or second century AD

109　A pair of bronze wrestlers or acrobats, probably intended for burial and the entertainment of the deceased in the after-life. It is the most remarkable essay in the representation of persons which has survived from pre-Han China. Fifth or fourth century BC

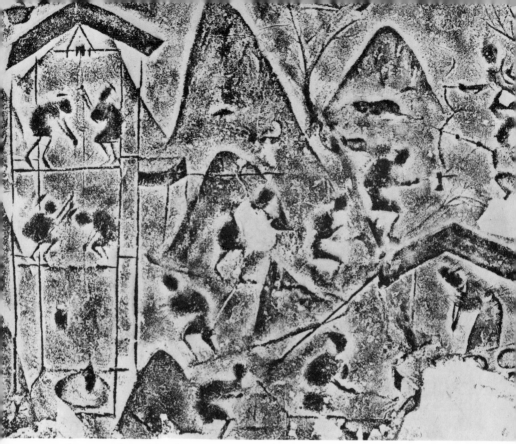

110 An unusual example of Han pictorial art in the form of a rubbing from a decorated brick of the first or second century A D. Salt miners and hunters are shown. Salt was first obtained by drilling, using the derrick on the left of the picture. Dissolved in water, it was then dried out in the pans on the right. Beyond, hunters are shooting game with crossbows

Ill. 106
Ills. 112, 113
smaller bronzes. In the decoration of harness trappings, belt-hooks (from the third century B C), and mirrors (from the fourth century B C) the Chinese genius for powerful expression through narrowly prescribed forms is no less apparent.

Ills. 114–118
The abundance of bronze mirrors found in graves from the fourth century B C onwards is probably owed to a superstition which became part of Taoist lore. The idea is expressed as follows in a book purporting to be the sayings of the alchemist and pharmaceutist Pao P'u Tzŭ, compiled in the fourth century A D:

111 A bronze ritual bell, *chung*, of the early fifth century BC. The quality of the casting puts the bell among the best work of the Chinese bronze casters of any period

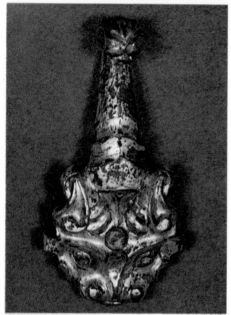

112, 113 Belt-hooks were introduced into China at some time in the fifth century BC, being copied from the dress of the mounted nomads who inhabited the north-western area. Both examples are of bronze, the one shown above is inlaid with turquoise. Often fantastic animals are depicted, as left, in a style known as 'chip-carving'. Belt-hooks of this style are usually gilded

'The essences of the ancient things of creation are all capable of assuming human shape and can deceive men's eyes by the illusion; and often they put mankind to the test. However, they are unable to change their true form in a mirror. Therefore when the Taoist masters of ancient times entered the mountains, they all hung at their backs a mirror measuring nine ts'un or more in diameter.'

Some primitive mirrors can be dated to the Shang period, when they already sketch the later invariable form: a disc of bronze with a central perforated knob on the

114, 115 The decorated backs of two
bronze mirrors of the late Chou
dynasty and the Han dynasty. The
design on the example above illus-
trates a cosmological scheme, con-
ventionally called the 'TLV pattern'.
The precise meaning of the symbols is
not completely known. The long
inscription mentions the manufacture
and the animal decoration. The mirror
to the right has a scrolled design in
which bird heads are combined with
rhomboid figures originating from
woven design. Textile patterns were
pervasive throughout Han decoration,
being cast in metal and painted in
lacquer

116–118 Beautiful ornament covers the backs of bronze mirrors of the late Chou and Han periods. *Ill. 116*, above left, of the early third century AD, shows the Taoist gods Hsi Wang Mu (Queen Mother of the West) and Tung Wang Kung (King Lord of the East), with a carriage and horses and a cavalry fight. *Ill. 117*, above right, of the first century AD, has a pattern of mythological animals and cosmological symbols. *Ill. 118*, left, of the late third or the second century BC, is decorated with phoenixes on a background of flowers and scrolling

back. The back of the mirrors of the classical period after 400 BC became a vehicle for striking designs, which in the Han period, under the influence of astrology and Taoist notions, were endowed with simple cosmological symbolism. The pre-Han mirror decoration generally has a ground pattern of the hook and volute motif which was pervading the bronze art as a whole (the so-called Shou Hsien group), or a diaper of small spirals, triangles, hachurings (the Loyang group). In the Shou Hsien mirrors the ground is overlaid with T-shaped or rhomboid figures, petalled flowers, spiralled leaping monkeys, birds, etc. The Loyang mirrors favour for the most part

Ill. 115

Ill. 114
Ills. 116–118

119–121 Jade carving first flourished in the Shang period and survives to modern times as a leading craft in China. Right and below left are a human mask and a stylized owl both probably intended as dress ornaments. Below right, a vertical pillar, the *tsung*, a pillar form combining circle and square, was later taken to be a symbol of the earth

122, 123 Many fine jade ornaments have been found, as illustrated opposite, but sets of jades forming a composite ornament are extremely rare. The necklace, right, consists of ten pieces, of which four are large milky grey, light green and brown jade pendants. The whole is strung together by a braided gold wire. It is said to come from a grave at Loyang, Honan province, of the late Chou dynasty, probably fourth century BC. The pieces shown in *Ill. 122* are of the tenth to sixth centuries BC

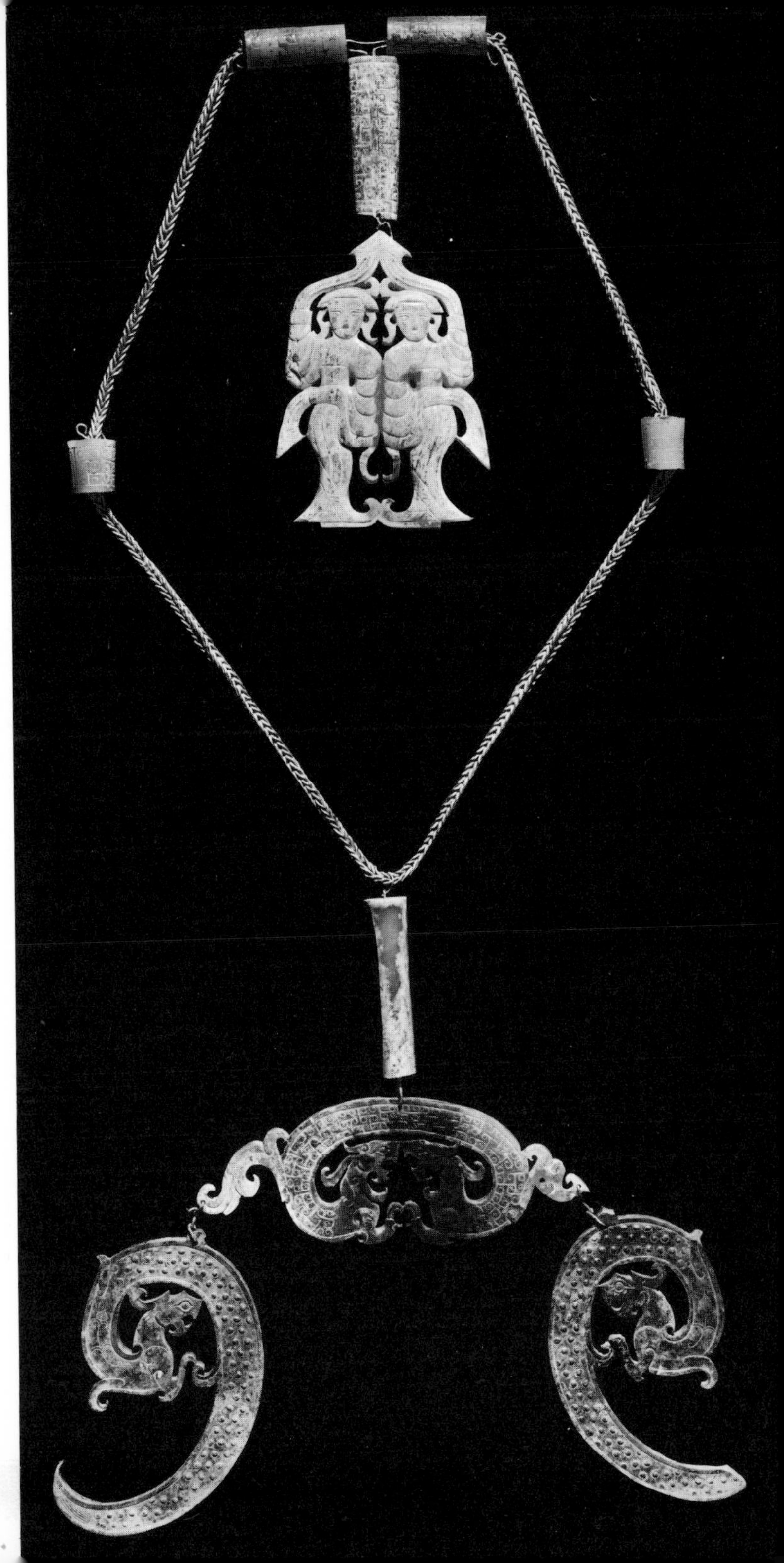

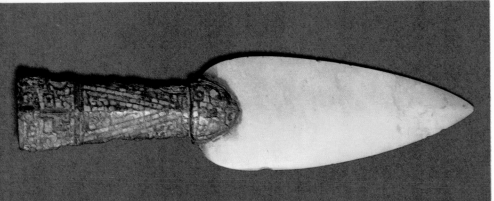

124–126 The use of large jade objects in ceremonial is described in ritualist texts dating from the late Chou and the Han periods. The large pierced circular discs, *pi*, were used by the emperor when performing sacrifices to heaven. The example opposite has an overall 'grain pattern' with pacing dragons coiled at the centre and standing away from the outer rim. The ornament of the *pi* above consists of an outer relief band of nine convoluted animal forms with bird and tiger heads. The inner zone has ten concentric circles of interlocking paired hooks. *Ill. 125*, opposite, is a ceremonial spearhead, having a white jade blade fitted into a bronze socket inlaid with turquoise mosaic. Thirteenth or twelfth century BC

a procession of leaping dragons of astonishing vigour, or dismembered, elongated and interlaced versions of them which turn into abstract patterns. The dragon-scroll mirrors of the second century BC appear to descend from the Loyang mirrors, but their compact figures lose something of the taut grace of the earlier designs.

The carving of jade, perhaps the most characteristic of all the crafts of ancient China, has a history extending from the Shang dynasty. Already in Neolithic times green and brown jade is found placed in graves in the form of miniature axes and rings, particularly in the region of the painted pottery. Whether a source of the stone existed in China itself is still uncertain. Most probably the ancient supply, like that of later times and of the present day, came from the rivers and mountains of Yankand and Khotan in Chinese Turkestan. In the Shang dynasty jade was used in *Ills. 119, 120* the manufacture of amulets representing imaginary birds, tigers, fish, hares, etc. These were mostly inscribed in silhouette on thin slabs, only the more elaborate pieces receiving any additional design or ornament on the surface. There are signs that the drilling and cutting was effected by thong or cord armed with an abrasive powder. *Ill. 121* The largest jades were the ritual objects: the *tsung*, a longitudinally perforated rectangular pillar, later designated *Ills. 124, 126* a symbol of earth by the ritualists; the *pi*, a disc with a wide central perforation, with which (in the Chou period at least) the emperor performed sacrifice to heaven. *Ill. 58* Oblong tablets (*hu*) and beautifully fashioned jade versions *Ill. 127* of halberd blades were other ritual objects. A few orna- *Ill. 125* mental spearheads have been found having a jade blade fitted to a bronze socket.

In the late fifth to early fourth century BC there was a revival of jade carving as fine craft. Improved methods of cutting and drilling appear to have been adopted at this time, for the jade carver succeeded in making such intricate patterns as the hook and white diaper, which is

127 A white jade copy of a halberd, *ko*. Such copies are found buried in tombs of the Shang dynasty

best known to us by its ubiquity in fine bronze. Jade carving rose to a level of perfection comparable to the gem cutting of ancient Persia and Greece. The *pi* and some ritual tablets were still made (the time was that of the Confucians' reinstatement of ancient ritual) but other pieces were frankly ornamental, such as elaborate pendants for necklaces, and ornamental archers' rings. The last decades of the third century BC saw the rise of fine lacquer-craft. It was this craft, rather than those of jade and bronze, which in the Han dynasty embodies the most striking legacy of the past. The Han lacquer workshops made bowls and wine-cups decorated with geometric

Ill. 134

Ills. 122, 123

Ills. 128–130

128, 129 Lacquer is only preserved in China in favourable conditions such as the waterlogged sandy soil of Ch'ang Sha and at Lolang in Korea (*cf. Ill. 107*). The lid above, brightly coloured and with three demon figures comes from the tomb of Wang Kuang at Lolang. The lacquer shield, left, was excavated from a tomb at Ch'ang Sha. The lacquer is painted on a base of leather mounted on a wooden frame

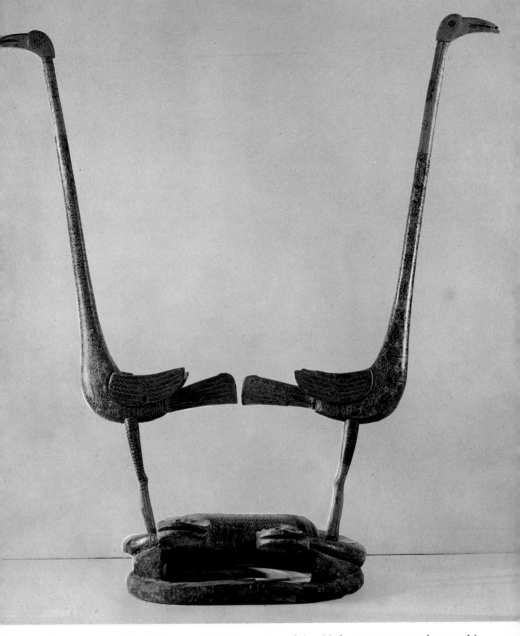

130 These cranes with their feet encircled by snakes, of the third century BC, are decorated in brightly coloured lacquer pigments. The meaning of this subject is not known, but the intention is more than ornament

131 Numerous pottery models have been found in tombs of the Han period. This example shows a farmhouse with a dog and a sheep in the courtyard. It comes from a tomb of the first century AD

patterns painted in gay red and yellow. The ones known to us were controlled by the state and their products were used for epicene gifts. In these circumstances a conservative adherence to a past artistic style is not unexpected. The new Han styles broke at last with the geometrized conventions of the ancient tradition. The first great cycle in the history of Chinese art was ended, and now appeared the first signs of the decorated naturalism which the modern eye sees as most characteristically Chinese. Clay models and stone reliefs of Han date transmit to us also the first representations of wooden buildings endowed with the essential Chinese characteristics.

Ills. 131–133

132 A tomb model of a tower-house of the Han dynasty. Such buildings supplied the idea of the pagoda tower which was later adopted into the architecture of Buddhist temples

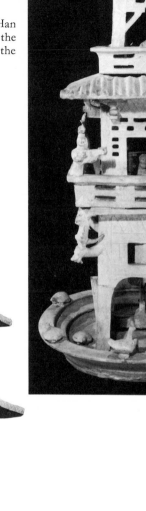

133 The model houses found in tombs of the Han dynasty give useful evidence of architectural styles of wooden buildings which have not survived from this early time

134 A fine example of a bronze dagger of the Chou period. Openwork casting of this quality is comparatively rare

Conclusion

The rigorously centralized administration created by Shih Huang Ti after the unification of 221 BC laid the basis of a social and political order destined to survive until modern times. New laws were imposed by draconian methods at first, according to principles advocated by the Legalist philosophers of the day, and a vain attempt was made to stamp out Confucianism at a blow by a burning of books. But Confucianism had become the code of the official class, and despite the Taoist leanings of some emperors and the advent of Buddhism its position was unshakeable. In the Han period too Chinese power began to extend into central Asia and Indo-China, where for the first time contact was made with traders of the Roman Empire.

Bibliography

History

CREEL, H. G. *The Birth of China: a Survey of the Formative Period of Chinese Civilization*. London, 1936

EBERHARD, W. *A History of China*. London, 1950

HERRMANN, A. *Historical and Commercial Atlas of China*. Cambridge, Mass., 1935

MASPERO, H. *La Chine antique*. Paris, 1927

Archaeology

ANDERSSON, J. G. *Children of the Yellow Earth*. London, 1934

CHENG TÊ-K'UN. *Archaeology in China*
     I: *Prehistoric China*. Cambridge, 1959
     II: *Shang China*. Cambridge, 1960

LI CHI. *The Beginnings of Chinese Civilization*. Seattle, 1957

WATSON. w. *Archaeology in China*. London, 1960
   China before the Han dynasty. London, 1961. For full bibliography
   Ancient Chinese Bronzes. London, 1962
   Handbook to the Collections of Early Chinese Antiquities in the British Museum. London, 1963

Weapons

LOEHR, M. *Chinese Bronze Age Weapons*. Ann Arbor, Michigan, 1956

Arts

BACHHOFER, L. *A Short History of Chinese Art*. London, 1944

WILLETTS, W. *Chinese Art*. London (2 vols.), 1958
   Foundations of Chinese Art. London, 1965

Mythology and Ritual

GRANET, M. *Danses et légendes de la Chine ancienne*. Paris, 1926

KARLGREN, B. 'Legends and Cults in Ancient China' in *Bull. Mus. Far Eastern Antiquities, Stockholm*, XVIII, 1946

WATERBURY, F. *Early Chinese Symbols and Literature: Vestiges and Speculations*. New York, 1942

Collections and Exhibitions

JENYNS, S. *Chinese Archaic Jades in the British Museum*. London, 1951

LODGE, J. E., WENLEY, A. G., and POPE, J. A. *Chinese Bronzes Acquired during the Administration of John Ellerton Lodge*. Freer Gallery of Art, Washington, 1946

YETTS, W. P. *The Cull Chinese Bronzes*. London, 1939

List of Illustrations

The author and publishers are grateful to the many official bodies, institutions and individuals mentioned below for their assistance in supplying original illustration material. Illustrations without acknowledgement are from originals in Thames & Hudson's archives.

52 Tomb wall painting of a hunt at T'ung-kou, Manchuria

53 Ritual halberd with jade blade and bronze socket. Shang-Ying period, c. 1766–1122 BC. British Museum. Photo John Freeman

54 Bronze halberd blade. Shang dynasty. British Museum. Photo John Freeman

55 Ritual halberd with jade blade and bronze socket. Late Shang or Early Chou dynasty. British Museum. Photo John Freeman

56 Bronze halberd with finial and ferrule. British Museum. Photo courtesy of the Trustees of the British Museum

57 Bronze halberd with ram's head decoration. Shang dynasty. British Museum. Photo Eileen Tweedy

58 Jade knife. Freer Gallery of Art, Washington, D.C.

59 Bronze ritual axe. British Museum. Photo Eileen Tweedy

60 Shang chariot burial from Ta Ssŭ K'ung, near Anyang, Honan province. Photo courtesy of the Britain–China Friendship Association

61 Chariot burials at Shang Ts'un Ling. Honan province. Chou dynasty

62 Reconstruction drawing of a chariot from Liu Li Ko. Drawn by Phillip Ward

63 Chariot burial at Liu Li Ko. Photo courtesy of the Britain–China Friendship Association

64 Iron edge of a spade from Ku Wei Ts'un. Drawn by Phillip Ward

65 Two-piece iron mould from Hsing

Lung Hsien. Photo courtesy of the Britain–China Friendship Association

66 Single-edged sword. British Museum. Photo courtesy of the Trustees of the British Museum

67 Classical Chinese sword. British Museum. Photo courtesy of the Trustees of the British Museum

68 'Antennae' hilt sword. British Museum. Photo courtesy of the Trustees of the British Museum

69 Sword-hilt with silk-bound hilt. British Museum. Photo courtesy of the Trustees of the British Museum

70 Bronze crossbow mechanism. British Museum. Photo courtesy of the Trustees of the British Museum. The crossbow mechanism drawn by Phillip Ward

71 Bronze *ting*. Shang dynasty. Ashmolean Museum. Photo John Webb

72 Bronze *kuei*. Early Chou dynasty. British Museum. Photo A. C. Cooper

73 Bronze *chia*. Early Shang dynasty. British Museum. Photo John Freeman

74 Bronze *chia*. Shang dynasty. British Museum. Photo Eileen Tweedy

75 Bronze *kuei*. Shang-Chou period. Captain Dugald Malcolm collection. Photo Eileen Tweedy

76 Bronze *tsun*. Shang dynasty. British Museum. Photo Eileen Tweedy

77 Bronze horse frontal. British Museum. Photo John Freeman

78 Gold openwork dagger hilt. British Museum. Photo Eileen Tweedy

79, Gold and silver inlaid bronze
80 chariot fittings. British Museum.
Photo Eileen Tweedy

81 Bronze *fang-yi*. Shang dynasty.
Courtesy of the Smithsonian Institution, Freer Gallery of Art, Washington D.C.

82 Shang dynasty bronze ritual vessel
types. Drawn by Phillip Ward

83 Set of bronze ritual vessels from Feng
Hsiang, Shensi province. Courtesy
of the Metropolitan Museum of Art,
Munsey Bequest, 1924

84 Bronze *tui*. Late Chou dynasty.
Courtesy of the Fogg Art Museum,
Harvard University

85 Bronze double *fu*. Eastern Chou
dynasty. Photo courtesy of the Art
Institute of Chicago

86 Bronze *yü*. Shang dynasty. Hakutsuru
Museum, Kobe

87 Bronze *yü*. Shang dynasty. Photo
courtesy of the Musée Cernuschi,
Paris

88 Bronze *yü*. Shang dynasty. Courtesy
of the Smithsonian Institution,
Freer Gallery of Art, Washington
D.C.

89 Bronze *ku*. Shang dynasty. British
Museum. Photo John Freeman

90 Bronze *ho*. Shang dynasty. Courtesy
of the Smithsonian Institution, Freer
Gallery of Art, Washington D.C.

91 Bronze *yi*. Early Chou dynasty. Mrs
W. Sidgwick collection, London

92 Bronze *chih*. Early Shang dynasty.
Ashmolean Museum, Oxford

93 Bronze *hu*. Chou dynasty. Victoria
and Albert Museum

94 Chou dynasty pottery types. Drawn
by Phillip Ward

95 Bronze *kuang*. Shang dynasty.
Courtesy of the Smithsonian Institution, Freer Gallery of Art, Washington D.C.

96 Ordos bronze, horses fighting.
British Museum. Photo courtesy of
the Trustees of the British Museum

97 Ordos bronze, wolf attacking a
horse. British Museum. Photo
courtesy of the Trustees of the
British Museum

98 Ordos bronze, two ibexes. British
Museum. Photo courtesy of the
Trustees of the British Museum

99 Bronze belt-hook. British Museum.
Drawn by Phillip Ward

100, Bronze human figure. William Rock-
101 hill Nelson Gallery of Art, Kansas
City

102 Decorated bronze axe-head. British
Museum. Photo Eileen Tweedy

103 Inlaid and decorated spearhead.
British Museum. Photo Eileen
Tweedy

104 Brick tomb in the eastern suburb of
Canton. Drawn by Phillip Ward

105 Pottery model boat from Canton.
Canton Museum. Photo courtesy of
the Britain–China Friendship
Association

106 Bronze openwork ornament. Photo
courtesy Britain–China Friendship
Association

107 Lacquered basket from Lolang,
Korea. Seoul Museum. Photo
courtesy Heibonsha Kabushiki
Kaisha, Tokyo

108 Three glazed pottery figurines playing *liu po*. British Museum. Photo John Freeman

109 Bronze pair of wrestlers. Formerly Captain G. Spencer-Churchill collection. Photo Peter Clayton

110 Rubbing from a decorated brick in the Szechwan Provincial Museum. Photo John Freeman

111 Bronze *chung*. Chou dynasty. Museum voor Aziatische Kunst, Amsterdam

112 Bronze inlaid belt-hook. Third century BC. British Museum. Photo Eileen Tweedy

113 Bronze gilt belt-hook. Third century BC. British Museum. Photo Eileen Tweedy

114 Bronze mirror back. Shou Hsien style, fourth to third century BC. British Museum. Photo Peter Clayton

115 Bronze mirror back. Han dynasty, second century BC. Ashmolean Museum. Photo Eileen Tweedy

116 Bronze mirror back. Third century AD. British Museum. Photo John Freeman

117 Bronze mirror back. First century AD. British Museum. Photo John Freeman

118 Bronze mirror back. Late third or second century BC. British Museum. Photo John Freeman

119 Jade human mask amulet. Tenth to eighth century BC. British Museum. Photo Eileen Tweedy

120 Jade owl amulet. Thirteenth to eleventh century BC. British Museum. Photo courtesy of the Trustees of the British Museum

121 Jade ritual *tsung*. Shang dynasty. British Museum. Photo courtesy of the Trustees of the British Museum

122 Jade pendants and amulets. Probably Chou dynasty. Formerly C. T. Loo collection

123 Jade necklace. Late Chou dynasty. Courtesy of the Smithsonian Institution, Freer Gallery of Art, Washington D.C.

124 Pierced jade *pi*. Late Chou dynasty. William Rockhill Nelson Gallery, Kansas City

125 Jade ceremonial spearhead. Shang dynasty. British Museum. Photo Eileen Tweedy

126 Pierced jade *pi*. Late Chou dynasty. Art Institute of Chicago

127 Jade *ko*. Shang dynasty. British Museum. Photo courtesy of the Trustees of the British Museum

128 Lacquered lid from Lolang. Seoul Museum

129 Lacquered shield from Ch'ang Sha

130 Pair of lacquered birds. Cleveland Museum of Art

131 Pottery model farmhouse. British Museum. Photo John Freeman

132 Tomb model of a tower. Han dynasty. Courtesy of the Fogg Art Museum, Harvard University

133 Tomb model of a house. Han dynasty. William Rockhill Nelson Gallery of Art, Kansas City

134 Bronze dagger and scabbard. Chou dynasty. British Museum. Photo Peter Clayton

Index